Discovering the Soul

"Dr. Jarmon, a renowned psychiatrist, describes his patients' encounters with their souls and, in doing so, shows the lay reader and the therapist alike how working with such concepts can be just as real and often more effective than any other modern psychotherapeutic approach."

> Gerald Jampolsky, M.D.
>
> Author of *Love Is Letting Go of Fear*

"With the skill of a consummate storyteller, Dr. Jarmon has forged an important new chapter in the history of medical hypnotherapy. He writes with candor, clarity, and courage, providing answers to questions for those of us who find traditional views inadequate."

> Irene Hickman, D.O.
>
> Author of *Mind Probe Hypnosis* and
>
> *Remote Depossession*

"A wise and well-informed psychiatrist has taken the time to really listen to what his patients are saying. The stories they told helped him to guide their healing, spiritually. Psychiatry literally means treatment of the psyche, and *psyche* means soul. Thank you, Dr. Jarmon, for this insightful book that integrates the concept of the soul in treating patients."

> Daniel A. Zelling, M.D.
>
> Past Editor-in-Chief,
>
> *American Journal of Hypnoanalysis*

Discovering
the Soul

The Amazing Findings of
A Psychiatrist and His Patients

by Robert G. Jarmon, M.D.
with a Foreword by
Raymond A. Moody, Jr., M.D.

Library of Congress Cataloging-in- Publication Data
Jarmon, Robert G.
Discovering the soul : the amazing findings of a psychiatrist and his patients
by Robert G. Jarmon
Includes bibliographical references.
1.Hypnotic age regression-Therapeutic use-Case studies. I.Title RC499.H96J37 1996
616.89'162-DC20   96-38945

Dedication

This book is dedicated to all of those other souls making part of my journey with me so that I can learn what I need to learn, and do whatever it is that I am supposed to do during this lifetime.

Especially to my father, Albert Jargowsky, for the fun lessons, to my mother, Helen Pisarowicz, for the difficult lessons, and to *their* parents who had the moxie and the *chutzpah* to leave Eastern Europe so we could grow in a better place. And to my wife, Mary, for making the journey a joy.

Special Thanks

I would like to thank my good friends and colleagues who gave of their time and talents, critiquing and encouraging this work: Suzanne Carmody, R.N., Robert Elman, and Richard and Deborah Herr.

A special belated and ongoing thanks to that dreaded, New England bred, tough little old lady schoolmarm English teacher at Long Branch High School, Miss Tilley. Nobody wanted to be in her class (and I had her twice!). She was ruthless in tearing apart our compositions, and she was one of the finest teachers I ever had. Over half a century later I cannot sit down to write so much as an email without imaging her looking over my shoulder admonishing, "Too many words... Lacks parallelism... Mixed tenses... Redundant... If it's a sentence, end it with the appropriate punctuation... "Thing" is a lazy word. Tell the reader what the *thing* is... Superfluous... Sentence is too long, break it up...You just used that word, find a synonym"!

I wish we still had a lot of teachers like her. When I hear

talk about evaluating good teachers for merit pay raises, the last criteria I want to hear is whether or not the current students like that person. Ask them later, in about half a century. And, BTW, regarding all those mistakes in grammar and punctuation which got past me in this book – it's your fault Miss Tilley for not being even tougher.

Contents

Foreword

The opportunity to write the foreword for this book has come to me through a fortuitous triangulation of wonderful people whom I love. The author, Dr. Bob Jarmon, has been a friend for years. I got to know him through Dr. Brian Weiss in conjunction with our speaking engagements at the Association for Research and Enlightenment (A.R.E.), in Virginia Beach, Virginia. Bob is a fine, thoughtful person with great common sense. As medical doctors, people like to keep us in pigeonholes, but since I have so much fun exploring new ideas, I'm often in hot water with the old guard.

In this brief foreword, I am hereby declaring my own independence from the old ways of arguing and disputing about the paranormal. What passes for scholarship about this subject seldom makes any real progress. The fact is that the controversy has been deadlocked since antiquity. The very framework of argumentation has been inadequate, apparently monopolized by three schools of thought. Modern parapsychologists struggle to fulfill the false promise that someday the scientific method, or some other rational procedure, will "prove" or provide empirical evidence for life after death, ESP, or precognition. The "scientific skeptics," who aren't really skeptics at all, are otherwise well-meaning scientists who think they have all the answers; paranormal experiences, they believe, are easily explainable as wishful thinking, hoaxes, or mixed-up brain chemistry. The third category comprises those fundamentalists of philosophical and religious thought, who, through self-righteous judgment, would condemn anyone who dares to explore the paranormal, searching for demons behind every unexplainable phenomenon.

The fact is that all three groups have shared equally in their inadequacy to discover the truth about the paranormal.

Aside from their inherent prejudices, the use of inadequate language has been primary among their impediments. What has been required, and quietly unfolding over the past several years, has been a new breed of investigator, one who has all the benefits of a scientific education, along with spiritual honesty, and open minded inquiry. Here, I cite the work of Dr. Weiss, my own contribution, whatever that may be, and, of course, the work of Dr. Jarmon.

With my techniques of recreating paranormal experiences, and the cutting edge work presented in this book, the day is fast approaching when people will no longer need to get their information about the paranormal second-hand, by hearing it from others. There will one day be a system in place that will enable everyone to observe their own paranormal experiences. Ordinary people will be in a position to make up their own minds about the paranormal, and at that point the three stuffy old systems of thinking about the paranormal will be obsolete. We will no longer have to hear about it from the "experts"; we will have our own personal experiences upon which to reflect.

Dr. Jarmon's book is a good example of the new direction in which the study of the paranormal is moving. What he writes is a plain demonstration that we ordinary folk can recognize and understand life-changing, paranormal, and spiritual experiences. I like his way of proceeding: show people that the paranormal is accessible, and permit them to open up to the extraordinary alternate realities that are an important part of being human.

Thanks again to Bob Jarmon and Brian Weiss. I'm looking forward to our continuing friendship for a long time to come.

Raymond Moody, M.D.

Preface

As a physician writing a book on psychotherapeutic techniques, I was warned to not use the word God, as that would undermine my credibility and risk making me sound like an evangelist in sheepskin clothing. My apologies to those who take offense at the "G" word, but I could find no legitimate or convenient way around it. I toyed with trying to give God a scientific pseudonym such as "Universal Energy Pool," the "Omni Factor," the "Ubiquitous Cosmic Force Field," etc., but all of those terms seemed blatantly too cumbersome. So "God" it is.

As you read this book and I share with you my observations and thoughts about giving attention to the soul in psychotherapy, some of you will undoubtedly find yourselves skeptical or even taking offense as science attempts to trod on religion's turf. In my practice the questions that often arose with this treatment approach relate to religious heresy, scientific provability, and therapeutic efficacy.

As to the first concern, whether or not a person is labeled a heretic or infidel is, of course, purely a function of who is doing the labeling.

As to the second concern, much if not all of this theory evades scientific methodology (as is true of most of what we take for granted as valid).

As to the last concern, "Does this really work?" the answer is a resounding . . ."often."

Introduction

This book is about an alternative way that modern psychotherapy could deal with mental illness. When I was about to graduate medical school in 1973, I had two major interests, emergency medicine and psychiatry. I liked the excitement and rapid results of the first, but also the analysis and emotional healing of the second. I had become particularly intrigued with the concept of ESP and souls, and how they might play a part in psychotherapy. When I interviewed for psychiatry residencies and brought up those interests, I was uniformly advised that rigorous psychiatric training would squash such naive notions. That's not what I was looking for. I graduated first in my medical school class in the field of psychiatry and decided to go into the new specialty of emergency medicine.

During the following years and through my work in the E.R., I occasionally came across hints at this esoteric and elusive nature of the psyche, which only served to further stimulate my curiosity. Some of those incidents will be described in this book. After about fifteen years in emergency medicine, I was becoming cynical and burnt out. It was time to move on.

For most of those E.R. years I was also seeing patients in a small side practice I had in hypnotherapy. It started out as a way to help people get off cigarettes, but I soon found there were a lot of people who just wanted to talk out their problems with a physician, as long as that physician was not a "psychiatrist". The old line, "You'd have to be crazy to see a psychiatrist" came up more than once. I had kept up with my readings in psychiatry and had taken some extra course work, always with an eye towards taking on a psychotherapy practice full-time. After fifteen years of twelve hour shifts in *blitzkrieg* E.R. medicine in which I had to get a good working handle on the emotional makeups of dozens of patients and their families, I had a lot of practice in reading people and their problems.

I used those skills of rapid assessment and clinical hypnosis, along with a handful of psychotropic medications, to help people gain insight. Most patients I dealt with were intelligent enough to know the solution to their problems, once they were able to step outside of themselves and look back. The reason most people are better at giving advice to a friend than to themselves, is because they can be more objective, not because they are necessarily smarter.

This book is about the soul and some of its interactions in psychotherapy. I am not going to discuss the long-accepted principles and theories of psychiatry, psychoanalysis, or the contributions of such pioneers as Freud, Jung, Adler, and others whose beliefs were disdained at one time as metaphysical "nonsense." I would like to share what I have experienced with the nature of the soul, or spirit; about the survival of the spirit after death; and its manifestations and re-appearance in successive lives.

I will also discuss the applications of these concepts in my approach to psychiatric healing, often in conjunction with the now more widely accepted tools of hypnoanalysis and hypnotic regression.

I will describe therapy sessions in which hypnotic regression enabled patients to relive the positive and negative experiences of childhood and early infancy. Some patients appeared to regress *beyond their present lives to past lives.* In doing so, they came to understand and conquer mysteries, disorders, or deeply troubled feelings that had plagued them for years.

Whether the underlying concepts of the soul and the afterlife can ever be definitively confirmed (or are even valid) may be irrelevant to healing effectiveness. If therapy works, it works, and I am not talking about simply covering up a symptom while the underlying problem still exists. And for these patients it worked.

Certainly, not all problems are purely or even mostly spiritual in nature. There are many psychiatric disorders which require very well-established therapeutic interventions, and some disorders are incurable, some sufferings unavoidable. Yet, it is also true that the mind, spirit, and emotions strongly influence a great many human disorders and illnesses, physical as well as mental, and the goal of healing ought to always be *total* healing.

I did not always follow this New Age, path. I came to it in gradual steps, first by studying and practicing psychiatry, then by adding hypnosis to my therapeutic arsenal, and finally encountering phenomena difficult if not impossible to explain in any terms but the spiritual.

The nature of the soul has always been and still is a mystery to me. My questions about it have changed through the years. At first I asked, is it real? Is it tangible, and if so, where is it located? Does it have a visible manifestation? What color is it? What happens to it when we die? Do animals have them? Are there people without souls?

Gradually, my questions became more sophisticated and "scientific." Does the soul represent a hitherto unmeasured energy wave form? Does it fit into any paradigm of traditional Newtonian physics? Is it merely a stratagem of the fearful mind, created by us to give hope for existence beyond inevitable death? If it does exist, what influence might it exert on a patient's physical or emotional health? Does it remain its own discrete entity, or as Thomas Edison believed it is more like a swarm of bees which can break up and reform into different shapes and with its individual members leaving and entering the group.

Another concept to consider is that of anachronistic archetypical behavior, that being one which we still manifest although its usefulness is long gone. Someone under hypnosis might imagine himself to be an ancient stone mason because such was part of our common human experience, and not because in a previous life his soul inhabited the body of a particular stone mason.

Every day waking examples of this happens when before your dog lies down on the den floor, he walks around in a circle. It's a throwback to when his ancestors who emerged from the tall grass savannahs of Africa needed to mat down the grass before they could be comfortable on it. Before he urinates on a tree, he will sniff it to see if the territory has already been staked out by another animal's urine in the wild. The human version of this is pee shyness, in which a man may have difficulty urinating if another man is standing next to him, because he has encroached on another's territory. And we all seem to enjoy the cozy feeling of cuddling up in front of a fire on a cold dark night, but why? It's not for the heat and the light. If we wanted that we would just turn up the thermostat and turn up the lights. It must be a throwback to what our ancient ancestors felt when having a controlled fire in front of them, they felt a measure of protection from the elements and the animals.

A major obstacle in acknowledging the existence of the soul, or spirit, in the construct of human pathology is the problem of measuring or quantifying it. Where under the microscope or at the autopsy table can a medical student see it? How can we even be sure it exists? I have heard many stories of dogs sensing the presence of some sort of spirit. Maybe we should hook up some of these animals with portable EEG monitors and go exploring? We use other human animal biomarkers to help quantify energy around us such as Scoville units (for rating pungency in hot peppers), decibels, and candle power.

Most of the time (though not always) the soul is invisible, which naturally arouses skepticism. If it can't be measured, how could it exist? But didn't barometric pressure exist before 1643 when Torricelli invented the barometer? Did ultraviolet and infrared light exist before we could measure them?

By the same logic, should I ignore a patient's accounts of

anything whose reality I cannot prove? Perhaps we should abandon analgesics with their potential adverse side effects. After all, I have never *seen* a patient's pain. If I cannot test and measure it objectively, and only take the patient's word for it, how can I know it exists?

Another problem in dealing with the concept of the soul is that by merely speaking of it we begin to sound like religious disciples or evangelists. Religion and medicine are supposed to have gone their separate ways centuries ago. No longer do most civilizations have their healers, who at one time ministered to the body and soul together, recognizing no clear delineation. Such healers are the equivalent of modern therapists who dare to look at the entire person, mind-body-spirit, and prescribe accordingly. The holistic approach is much more difficult today, although fortunately, there are therapists who practice it. One obstacle to it is sheer amount of medical knowledge, which has become too voluminous for any one practitioner to know in its entirety. We, therefore, tend to concentrate only on physical-observable, testable, or measurable aspects of a given problem, bringing to bear our specialized (thus limited) training. Other aspects, being harder to detect and harder still to comprehend, are ignored. But a patient is something more than a malfunctioning machine and we ought to be something more than mechanics.

Even the way we view the brain and its functions is open for debate. Studying neuro-anatomy in medical school, a student tends to get the impression that the brain is merely a complex matrix of neurons which also pumps out hormones, like a complex set of wires which excrete fluids. We can get a mechanistic perspective and confuse the brain with the mind. But this organ is also like a radio receiver, taking in and converting stimuli. Aside from the more commonly thought of stimuli such as sound and visual light, perhaps it is also a receiver for psychic energy. A human's ability here is not as good as a canine's, but then neither is our sense of smell.

Whether or not you accept the concepts in this book is up to you. Here, I present these case studies as I would to colleagues in a medical conference. All of these reports are real. I have only changed the details enough to maintain patient anonymity. We can treat the physical body, but eventually it will die. But when we can successfully treat the soul, the effects could be permanent.

Part I

How We Form
and Re-form Our Beliefs

Chapter 1

The Difficulties in Changing Our Minds

In the introduction to this book, I remarked that I was not always so spiritual in my clinical approach and I enumerated some impediments to the acceptance of the spiritual factor as a component of any problem to be treated. I wrote of skepticism, the limitations of classroom and clinical training, and the almost unmanageable amount of information that must be mastered by a medical practitioner even within a narrow field of specialization.

Within the incredibly vast amount of academic medical training to understand the complexities of the human condition there is virtually nothing about the soul, even though most physicians consider themselves to be religious or spiritual.

The fact that you have seriously considered reading this book indicates that you have a curious, searching mind, which is a key sign of intelligence. If you have ever changed your mind about a core concept you held, you are unlike many others who maintain the attitude, "My mind is made up, so don't confuse me with the facts." So if you are going to read this with the prospect that you might incorporate some of its ideas, you might find it useful to arm yourself with a checklist of what can get in the way of changing our minds. Some of the more common blocks people tell themselves are:

"I never heard that before.

Why should I believe that person...what are his/her credentials in this field?

My old way works well for me (for the most part).

My friends/colleagues/family/spiritual leader would think I'm crazy(-er).

It makes no sense to me (based on my frame of reference to date).

If I proclaimed an attitude like that it would threaten my job/standing/career.

If it can't be measured or repeated on command, it can't be real.

The old way is good enough for me, because it was good enough for...

That's never been my experience, so I can't believe it could be anyone else's either.

If I incorporated this new idea it would mean I would have to discard (almost) everything else I have believed in and which has always been my foundation."

Rarely does a single experience totally change a person's views of life, death, and the possibilities of all that lies before and after. Rather, there are cumulative effects on one's views, built on a foundation of many experiences. Some of these experiences may be as dramatic as the rainbow that marked my mother-in-law's passage to the afterlife. Others may be subtle and may even seem unimportant, if not trivial at the time they happen, but they add to our experiences and by that help to form our beliefs.

Then there was Carol.

Carol was a single, pleasant 28 year old woman who came to me for smoking cessation. As with all the other thousands of patients I dealt with for smoking she had reasons to quit as well as reasons or drives to not quit. My job was to help tip the balance towards permanently getting off the addiction. With young women, risks of emphysema or heart disease rarely carry much weight. So we often talk about bad breath, wrinkles, damage to fetuses, and trashy appearances. I always ask about influences of family and friends. Often a promise to an important relative, or the memory of one dying of a smoking related disease, can tip the scales. It turned out that in Carol's case, a promise she had made to her grandfather was the issue which brought her to counseling. But it turned out there was a lot more to her story.

Carol had been very close to her grandfather who had died four years earlier of emphysema. He had asked her to please quit smoking, but though she had promised him, she had been unable to break the addiction. I asked her why it was that now she was finally coming in for help. She told me that one night the previous week she had an extremely vivid dream. In that her grandfather appeared to her looking much younger than when he died. He said, "Carol, it's time to stop smoking". He was wearing an old style shirt that she had never seen before. He pointed to the shirt pocket. Then she suddenly woke up. In the morning she told her mother about the strange dream and how it seemed so real. She also wondered about that odd shirt and described it. Her mother said she vaguely remembered a shirt like that her father wore, and she wondered if he hadn't stored it away with his old army clothes in his attic trunk.

They went into the attic, pulled out the trunk, and found that shirt at the bottom of a pile of papers and old clothes. In the shirt pocket was a note in the grandfather's handwriting. The shirt was an old one he had thrown on when he took his daughter, Carol's mother, to the hospital to deliver Carol. He had written the note while waiting to see his first grandchild. In it he said how ecstatic he was about having a little granddaughter and how he prayed that her life would be filled with health, happiness, and love. Reading the note, the two women were speechless and teary-eyed. Carol needed no more incentive to finally try to quit smoking.

She got off and stayed off the cigarettes. My part had been easy since her grandfather had already done the work. Later I wondered how well-meaning, traditionally trained psychotherapists, who did not believe in the possibility of a spirit world, might have handled this case. Perhaps they would say Carol was simply a wishful thinker or a pathologic liar. Maybe she really wrote the note herself after carefully studying the old man's handwriting in an attempt to impress her gullible mother. Maybe Carol is a schizophrenic who thinks she has the power to communicate with the dead. And maybe what she really needs is some good, intensive psychoanalysis to get to the root of her true pathology.

The very laws of physics and thermodynamics that support a mechanistic view (to the exclusion of such mystical concepts as the spirit) hold that energy cannot be destroyed or obliterated, but only altered. We also know that the brain produces and works with electrical energy impulses and waves. If psychic energy exists and cannot become non-existent, what happens to this energy when its temporary housing, the body, ceases to maintain its metabolic functions? That is, what happens to that energy when we die?

Of course, there are many who do not believe that psychic energy exists in the first place. Since they have not experienced it in some manifestation, and no reputable scientist has yet devised a "psycho-meter" to demonstrate its reality, why embrace such a major and unconventional concept? I, for one, would not have until it presented itself to me in various ways. Now that it has, I cannot negate what I have witnessed.

It has been my experience that psychic energy does not invariably or necessarily await bodily death to be released and express itself outside of the confines of the body. It may take a variety of forms.

Before entering medical school, I had never considered myself (or perhaps anyone else) to possess any psychic abilities. I had, of course, read about extrasensory perception (ESP), telepathy, clairvoyance, and so on, but considered them nothing more than intriguing notions. More and more in recent years, investigative and law-enforcement agencies have successfully employed people with exceptional psychic abilities to locate missing persons or corpses, or find hidden evidence. But that was none of my experience. Then, shortly after I entered medical school, two occurrences challenged and broadened my system of beliefs in how the universe functions.

If a system of beliefs cannot accommodate challenge and potential change, it must be a weak and fearful system. The French essayist, Joseph Joubert, observed that "those who never retract their opinions love themselves more than they love truth." Gloria Steinem observed that "the first problem for all of us, men and women, is not to learn but to unlearn." My own convictions began to be unlearned during my medical student days.

A good friend, George Bundy, and I had been traveling together frequently, taking a series of airline flights, and now we were to fly from Miami to New York with a brief stop at Fort Lauderdale. As we walked along the airport concourse toward our boarding gate, I was suddenly overwhelmed by an intense feeling of foreboding. I **KNEW** with absolute certainty that the plane would not reach its final destination. I had not yet even seen the plane. Never before had I been nervous about flying, and the feeling of panic was all the stronger for being unfamiliar.

I grabbed George's arm and told him we must not board the plane but wait for the next flight. Then I saw the aircraft and my feeling of impending doom intensified even more. "There is something wrong with that plane," I told him, "some structural problem, and there's going to be trouble. I don't know how I know, but it's not going to get us to New York."

During the few minutes before boarding, he questioned me about what I "saw" or sensed. His questions served to focus my mental images more clearly, and I told him I saw no physical harm coming to us or any of the passengers and crew, but I knew the plane had some defect that would abort its flight.

"Come on," George said. "Even if your premonition comes true, you said you don't see anyone getting hurt. Our bags are on board, so let's go. I never knew you were afraid of flying, but this premonition of yours will make it interesting. And, since you say that we're not going to get hurt, don't you want to see what happens? Let's go."

So we boarded. When we took our seats, I still somehow knew that we would not be injured, yet, I had never in my life been so frightened. It was all the more bewildering because I never had a fear of flying. As I boarded the plane, a terror set in and that would not leave.

At Fort Lauderdale, we sat on the tarmac for thirty minutes then George glanced out the window and saw the baggage being unloaded. Soon we were ushered off the plane and told that we would be driven back to Miami, where we would resume our flight on another aircraft. Upon disembarking, we looked back and saw fuel pouring out of an apparently ruptured fuel tank. It was streaming back close to the jet engines.

There had been no outward sign that anything was wrong with that plane, and moreover, my premonition had taken hold before I had even seen it. At the time, I was undergoing no significant stress, and there was no "logical" explanation for my foreknowledge. Somehow, a message about a future event had come to me from an inanimate object! George could dismiss the occurrence as a bizarre, if admittedly unlikely coincidence, but I could not. The only conclusion I could draw was that this universe is somehow much more complicated than my college physics professor would have led me to believe.

About a year later, another such experience challenged and shook my "logical" world. While visiting friends for the weekend, I suddenly knew that someone had died at home. At the same time, I also knew that it was not a member of my family who had died, so I was equally bewildered as troubled.

I tried to concentrate, seeking to sense whether someone had died while visiting my family, but I immediately knew that was not the case. Our property included an apartment which we rented out. Slowly, I began to sense that it must be the tenant who had died, but the only strong sensation I felt was that *someone* had died.

When I arrived home, my mother told me that she had found the tenant dead in his car. None of us were aware that he even had an illness. But how could I have known that someone had died? How had that information reached me? What was the nature of the transmission unit, on what sort of wave form did the information travel? What energy source drove it, and what was it in me that received and recognized it? Such experiences are not uncommon, yet people often dismiss them, chiefly because they are too challenging to what we think we know.

I began to pay more attention to articles and books concerned with extrasensory perception. An article in *Newsweek* mentioned research being conducted on mental telepathy by Douglas Dean, a faculty member at Newark College of Engineering which was five blocks from my medical school. I phoned Dr. Dean and he invited me to come over with a friend and participate in an experiment.

My classmate, Buzz Berlin, and I took turns sitting in a room and silently reading, at timed intervals, material that was alternately boring and then emotionally charged. While one of us read, the other sat in an adjoining room and had his pulse continuously monitored and recorded. Afterward, the type of reacting material was compared to changes in heart rate, and the correlated results indicated that a transmission of emotion was occurring between the two of us, although the person monitored had no conscious knowledge of what the other person was reading.

To me, this was more evidence of psychic energy, an energy which is not addressed in physics texts, but is nonetheless real, present, and able to affect our lives. I had begun to question my conventional set of beliefs, to unlearn the old and learn the new, to change my mind.

Since then, I have observed manifestations of psychic energy in other forms. Those forms have included what may be called discarnate spirits, spiritual entities that survive the death of the body and either rest in peace in what we call "the hereafter" or, in certain instances, remain or return to reside in a different body. I have heard patients under hypnosis speak of things unknown to them in their present lives, information acquired, perhaps, in past lives, retained by the soul, and unconsciously or subconsciously retrieved from the soul now inhabiting a living body.

All of us are inclined to believe in those things which we are taught from infancy, which our responsible mentors, colleagues, and friends believe, which we see or experience for ourselves, and which fit neatly into our already established concepts (like pieces of a jigsaw puzzle that snap into place to complete a picture).

When Copernicus began his study of astronomy, everyone "knew" the sun revolved around the earth. The science of the times and Mother Church both taught this "fact," which appeared self-evident. Anyone could gaze at the morning and evening skies and see the sun making its great arc around the earth. Scientists and philosophers had built an entire body of knowledge around that Law of Nature, which dated back to at least 340 B.C. when Aristotle described it in his treatise, *On the Heavens.* In the second century A.D., Ptolemy confirmed and elaborated the same easily accepted concept, which the Church viewed as one of many proofs that the earth was the center of the universe and Man its master, subordinate only to God who had created Man in His image.

But then Copernicus, a Roman Catholic priest, studied the night sky and found that the movements of some heavenly bodies could not be explained on the basis of the accepted earth/sun relationship. Ironically, as far back as the third century B.C., several Greek philosophers had suggested that the earth and other

9

planets revolved around the sun, but their ideas had never been widely accepted. Copernicus reconsidered those ideas, adding to them his own observations and calculations, and from about 1510 to 1514 prepared a manuscript summarizing his new theory. He must have anticipated resistance to such a theory- even outrage among his ecclesiastical superiors- because he circulated the work only among friends, almost secretively. Over the next two decades, he continued his studies and gradually began to write and speak more openly about his theory. As expected there was resistance, probably all the greater because Copernicus came to realize and declare that even the sun was not the center of the universe but at some distance from it and far more immense than anyone had imagined.

The Church during the Renaissance was not, however, as resistant to new ideas as one might suppose. In 1533, Pope Clement VII granted permission for the publication of the principles Copernicus had expounded in lectures given in Rome. But even with the Pope's approval, Copernicus was hesitant, foreseeing quite accurately a reaction of dissent among both clergy and laity. His great and final work, *On the Revolutions of the Celestial Spheres,* was published in the year of his death, 1543, and it initiated the profoundly shocking reformation of scientific theory known as the Copernican Revolution.

While many philosophers and theologians scorned Copernican theory as fantasy, or worse, heresy, a few inquisitive minds investigated and came to accept the new ideas, just as a few today are willing to explore phenomena scorned by skeptics. One such man was Galileo Galilei, a mathematics teacher at the University of Padua, who had come to accept Copernican theory early in life. Galileo, too, was afraid of ridicule (as he stated in a letter to a pioneering astronomer, Johannes Kepler, in 1597) and refrained from public expression of his opinions. Although Galileo did not invent the telescope, he was one of the first to use one to study the skies where he saw proofs of the new doctrine.

By the time he gathered the courage to lecture and write about his findings, the Inquisition was at the height of its reactionary power, and the Church was waging a war of ideas and allegiance with the Protestant reform movement. In 1616 the Vatican issued a decree that Copernicanism was "false and erroneous." All the same, Galileo obtained papal permission to write about the "systems of worlds", Ptolemaic versus Copernican, and did so. His opponents in the Church declared that his writings would have worse consequences "than Luther and Calvin put together."

In 1633 Galileo was tried by the Inquisition, sentenced to house arrest, and forced to spend the remaining eight years of his life in seclusion. It was not until 1980 that the Vatican re-opened its assessment of Galileo's work. After twelve years of studying the matter, it determined in 1992 that Galileo was right, that indeed the earth rotated around the sun, and they forgave him.[1] We condemn the Inquisition not only for its cruelty but for its obstinate blindness, and yet, today we tend to be equally blind to concepts which do not fit the construct of our conventional set of beliefs.

It is as if every generation thinks it knows just about everything there is to know about the universe. Imagine that you had an information shoe box of the exact size to be filled with microchips containing all that we know about the universe today. Now try to imagine how much smaller a box we would need to contain all that mankind knew 100 years ago. For 200 hundred years ago, we would have required an even smaller box, and so on going back. So why should we think and act as if we believed that in one hundred years we won't need a larger box than we have now? But that is exactly what we tend to do with unexplained phenomena. We try to make it fit within our currently accepted dogma, but that's only good for a start.

One version of this thinking is what is known as **Occam's Razor** which advises "When given two explanations for the same thing, the simpler one is usually the correct one." Using that logic, two thousand years ago the data in the information box would have told you that lightening was caused by Zeus hurling lightning bolts – end of discussion.

Another analytical position is **Positivism**, which says "If something can't be proven empirically, it doesn't exist." Accordingly, temperatures did not exist until we had

---

[1] Owen Gingerich, "How Galileo Changed the Rules of Science," *Sky & Telescope,* March 1993, pp. 32-36.

thermometers.

What about fire-walking? Is it possible that ordinary people can step barefoot on coals heated to 1200 degrees Fahrenheit without burning their feet? Can most people believe that? Do *you?* It most definitely does not fit into the Newtonian/Cartesian view of the universe. Nevertheless, fire-walking is a reality which we will look at in the next chapter.

There are some concepts or ideas that we can comfortably accept without understanding them. Like most people, I believe in Einstein's declaration that $E=mc^2$, not that I understand it, but because a great many trustworthy authorities believe it, because its validity has been proven and put to use by scientists, but mostly because <u>it does not threaten my basic belief system.</u> Yet, if tomorrow a *New York Times* article announced that world-renowned nuclear physicists discovered that actually $E=mc^3$, I don't think that would trouble us much. We would accept that as readily as $E=mc^2$ because it had no relevance to our day-to-day existence. When I examine the collection of colorful wires and metal and plastic bits inside my portable radio, I do not understand that either. I do not fully understand how I can hear the evening news broadcast, but I know that the "magic" of the device is not magic, and do not feel that I have to understand how it works before I turn it on and use it.

Generally speaking, people who have encountered psychic energy believe in its existence, while those who have never encountered it do not. But there is some crossover of belief/non-belief. Sometimes we refuse to believe our own eyes and ears because the information received does not fit our accepted set of natural laws. An approach, by the way, that too often leads to poor and dishonest scientific study reporting. Most of the time we are quite willing to accept a concept as true because others do. How much of what you were taught in school about science or history did you actually go out and validate for yourself?

Most people in America today shrug off or scoff at the concept of reincarnation, yet, most of the rest of world believes in it. It is a tenet of the major Asian religions, especially Hinduism, Jainism, Sikhism, and Buddhism. So whether or not you believe in reincarnation probably comes down to which side of the

Pacific Ocean you happened to be born on. It is also a tenet of many sects such as the Druse, an offshoot of Islam. Reincarnation, or at the very least the survival of the soul, is stated or implied in Biblical passages, and is in accord with ancient Judaic tradition.

Kabbala, a partly oral and partly written system of Jewish mysticism, addresses the concept. Kabbala is a complex interpretation, or collection of interpretations, of the scriptures. The period of greatest activity in compiling and refining it lasted from the twelfth to the sixteenth century, but in its earliest form, the *Merkava,* flourished in Palestine in the first century A.D. The chief literary product of the *Merkava,* the *Sefer ha-bahir,* compiled in the twelfth century, specifically states the reality of the return of souls: reincarnation.

But what of early Christianity? In the Gospel according to St. John (Chapter One), priests of Jerusalem asked John the Baptist if he was the Prophet Elijah reincarnated, and he said he was not. But Mark presents him as Elijah returned, and Matthew [Chapter Three) emphatically identifies him as Elijah, "he that was spoken of by the prophet Isaiah", the herald of the Kingdom of God. There is no question that early Christians believed in spirits (such as the spirits of Moses and Elijah, mentioned in the New Testament), angels (mentioned in both Old and New Testaments), the survival of the soul (mentioned often), and its reincarnation. (In II Maccabees, Chapter Seven, there is an account of the martyrdom of a mother and her sons. As they are about to have their hands and feet cut off and their tongues cut out, one of the brothers steps forward, sticks out his tongue and hands and says, "It is from heaven that I received these; for the sake of His laws I disdain them; from Him I hope to receive them again.") Then, at the Council of Nicaea in 325 A.D., the powers that were attempting to standardize Christianity denied reincarnation and expunged references to it. Perhaps they saw in it potential needs of a new cult that might threaten an organized structured religion and that religion's hierarchy of authority.

The concept of transmigration of the soul did not die easily. A multitude of minds had been opened to it over many centuries. In the eleventh century, a large sect known as the Cathari or Cathars, an offshoot of Catholicism, arose in Western Europe largely in opposition to what they perceived as materialism and corruption in the Church. As their movement spread, it splintered into a number of sub-sects, all of which reinterpreted the scriptures in ways considered heretical. They agreed concerning some beliefs, disagreed about others, but Catharism in its various forms concurred in the reality of reincarnation. As a group, they were often called Albigensians or Albigenses (after Albi, one of their chief centers in the south of France). In 1208, Pope Innocent III enlisted the aid of French noblemen to eradicate the Albigensians, rewarding the aggressors by putting his blessing on lands they confiscated. A crusade was proclaimed, and an army ravaged Toulouse, massacring its inhabitants, both Cathar and Catholic.[2]

More physicians and scientific researchers are investigating spirit energy and related phenomena. In addition to Dr. Brian Weiss, author of *Many Lives, Many Masters,* Dr. Ian Stevenson of the University of Virginia and Dr. Joseph B. Rhine (whose work at Duke University and at the Institute for Parapsychology has again and again claimed international attention), there are Dr. Gertrude Schmeidler at the College of the City of New York; Dr. William J. Baldwin of the Center for Healing Relationships in Enterprise, Florida; Dr. Raymond Moody, who wrote the Foreword to this book; Larry Dossey, M.D., author of *Recovering the Soul;* and others.

Psychotherapy, however, does not easily lend itself to quantitative measurements and conclusions. Essentially, all theories are just working hypotheses. On the basis of training, experience, and observation, the practitioner makes an apparently logical assumption about the mechanics of behavior. If the problem is solved by putting that assumption or approach into action, it acquires healing value. The prospect of adding spirituality to the psychic components that must be addressed in psychotherapy sounds as if it might only add uncertainty to confusion. Moreover, making assumptions about how the soul or spirit operates, to say nothing of such concepts as spirit entities and angels, sounds dangerously close to trying to explain how God thinks and operates. The notion seems as futile and arrogant

---

[2] *Holy Blood, Holy Grail,* Michael Baigent, p. 49.

as the concept of an ant looking up from the floor of the Sistine Chapel and asking about Michelangelo's choice of colors. We, like the ants, are not smart enough to ask the questions, much less understand the answers if they were given to us. Still, it is our nature to wonder and to understand. By making full use of spiritual concepts in psychotherapy, we add another component to the healing which we are trying to achieve.

Spirit can underlie many behavioral mysteries and anomalies. Consider the frequently sharp diversity in personality between siblings. In focusing on whether genetics or environment is more important in determining personality or pathology, we may be overlooking a third piece of the puzzle: the soul with which a person is born, that has been developing through previous existences and experiences.

Just as every physical ailment has an emotional component, every emotional problem may have a spiritual component. There seems to be a growing trend to bring spirituality back into healing. Perhaps this is because the results of standard psychotherapy have been somewhat disappointing. Although the factors at play are not well understood, even the FDA does not require that the "mechanism of action" be fully comprehended before bringing a new product to market. It is enough that the therapy be "safe and efficacious."

Hippocrates said, "Nothing should be omitted in an art which interests the whole world, one which may be beneficial to suffering humanity and which does not risk human life or comfort."

Chapter 2

Lessons from a Fire-walk

In recounting some of my clinical and personal experiences, I hope make it clear that my work was a constant reminder of the unsolved and yet, *useful* mysteries surrounding our lives. In a way, the psyche may be viewed as a microcosm of the cosmos, which teems with phenomena that can be seen, experienced, even tested, but not fully explained by currently known or understood physical science. Many of these phenomena can be utilized in healing, while others are useful in demonstrating both the power of the psyche and the immensity of the still unexplained.

When working with therapeutic concepts not fully embraced by the medical community, caution is especially essential. *Primum non nocer,* do not harm, is the first rule of medicine. All the same, there must be enough latitude in the system for new, potentially useful modalities to be introduced. Caution implies doubt which is *not* precisely the same attitude as skepticism. Doubt, in turn, implies faith, and faith implies doubt; and there are times when faith can and should override doubt.

A surgeon may have complete faith in his ability to diagnose appendicitis and remedy it by excision; but until he opens the abdominal cavity and sees the appendix, he cannot truly *know* it is inflamed, he can only surmise. Only when the appendix is removed, biopsied, and the patient recovers does he truly know his diagnosis and therapy were correct. Until then, some doubt, however small, has existed and faith has, therefore, been required.

"If the impossible is possible, then certainly the difficult is do-able."

On a hot, humid August evening in 1990, I found myself sitting on a hard metal folding chair in an unfamiliar back room of a church parish center. The scene was common enough at parish centers. There was a big pot of weak coffee, stacks of doughnuts, and eighteen strangers, aged ten to sixty. But what brought us there was anything but usual. We intended to walk barefoot over a bed of hot coals. As I blotted my brow with a handkerchief and looked about at those people, I asked myself why in the world I had come here. Was curiosity, an impulse to accept a dare, or a challenge?

Those aspects played a part, but something much more important was involved. I believe that every person is an amalgam of body, mind, and spirit, and I worked to incorporate this concept into my psychiatric practice as well as my personal life. I say I *work* at it because doubts inevitably creep into one's belief system. While I continually supported my patients through emotional and physical ailments, I wanted to validate it for myself.

A colleague had told me about this meeting. She said "Bob, I think you need to see this firsthand, although I'm not so sure you'll want to participate. The point is, you are always entreating your patients to trust their well-being to a higher power. This is your chance to find out how you really feel about it."

Actually, I needed little persuasion. The practice of fire-walking had fascinated me ever since I first read about it. Fire-walk rituals or ceremonies have sprung up in isolated cultures around the world, usually as an affirmation of religious faith or spiritual power and protection. Such rituals have been practiced by Cherokees, Tahitians, Tibetans, Hawaiians, Vikings, and Greeks. Now the fire-walk was coming to Monmouth County, New Jersey. I wanted to do it not to prove my courage, the way a schoolboy accepts a dare, but because I felt the experience might provide valuable insights. Also, if I were to put more faith in the higher power, the higher power might put more faith in me and enable me to be more effective. Something inside me was insisting: this I will do.

So there we were, nineteen people from various walks of life, listening to a woman in her mid-thirties instruct us how to walk unharmed through the flames. For nearly three hours we sat and spoke about overcoming fears, facing life's challenges, breaking self-erected mental and physical barriers. Twice during this time we went outside to build and stoke a bonfire, using a quarter-cord of oak wood, and rake out a sixteen-foot walkway with the glowing embers. At last the instructor announced, "It's time. Everyone remove your shoes and socks. Now, this is the chant you'll sing to the beating of the drum as we all hold hands around the fire and take turns walking through it. Okay?"

"Okay?" I thought. "I'll chant whatever she wants me to, hold hands with anyone, and do whatever she wants, if it will get me across those hot coals!" She also warned us to NOT do the walk unless we believed that we could. If we tried to walk the hot coals believing that we *would* be burned, then we would be burned.

We did it. In fact, I walked down the 16 foot path three times. A reporter who was there to cover the story laid down his note pad and joined us, and he too walked over the red-hot coals. A mother and her quiet ten-year-old son skipped joyfully over the 1,200-degree embers, a miraculous sight. I can't imagine what problems would have been caused if that boy had been burned. But for the rest of his life that child will be undaunted by life's self-imposed limitations. After all, if you can walk unscathed through fire, life's other fears and obstacles will be much less daunting.

One person did burn his feet, and his painful experience contained a lesson. A forty-year old chiropractor, who had voiced misgivings throughout the evening, evidently defeated himself. I drove his car home for him because his feet were too burned to use the foot pedals, and I dressed his second degree burns. But he had seen the phenomenon, had witnessed others as they walked the coals without injury, and had come away not only knowing more about himself but about the potential physical effects of faith. With surprisingly firm resolve, he said he would try it again at the next opportunity.

His injuries and pain were a gift to the rest of us- the gift of reality. It is tempting after the fire-walk to disbelieve what you have just experienced, to chalk it up to some relatively easy explanation such as moisture protection from your feet or poor conductivity of the coals, or mass hypnosis, perhaps. Certainly it has nothing to do with moisture or heat-conductivity. It would be absurd to believe that either factor would protect eighteen people but fail for the nineteenth. Nothing I had learned in physics, psychology, or physiology could fully explain what had transpired.

My own assessment was that when I stepped onto the burning coals, I believed that somehow I was in harmony with the energies of the universe and I would be safe because of that relationship, as untold numbers of other firewalkers had been before me. My burn patient had tried but failed to believe that he would be protected, and therefore, he was not protected.

Among a sect of Thai Buddhists there are many people who regard themselves as "spiritual mediums," empowered to bless other believers with the protection of a higher power, and during an annual religious celebration, they affirm their faith by walking on fire and by piercing their flesh with knives, needles, or spikes. The fire does not burn them. Their pierced cheeks, chests, or arms bleed very little, and investigating physicians have been baffled by the speed with which the punctures close and heal. After a day or two, the wound scars are barely visible. Some clinical observers have hypothesized that this phenomenon is made possible by mass-hypnosis or self-hypnosis.

The hypothesis is not unreasonable. Chanting or dancing often precedes a fire-walk and may serve as a hypnotic aid; indeed, the Thai firewalkers appear to be in trance. Group action and cohesiveness appears to help people who have not walked the coals before, although many may eventually do it alone. Unquestionably, hypnosis encompasses effects and abilities untapped by most of us and not fully understood by any of us. I cannot say that the awe inspiring and baffling protection afforded by the faith of these people is *not* a form of hypnosis, or that the faith itself is not a form of hypnosis. Perhaps hypnosis includes an aspect of getting more in harmony with the energies all around us. As physicists have said of the atoms that compose us and any other particle of matter, everything is energy, though some of it is in the form of matter.

Perhaps we are not meant to understand all the laws of the universe, but that does not mean we should not attempt to put them to work. There are two courses which we can simultaneously take: one is to continue seeking answers; the other is to put to work principles not fully understood but empirically known to be safe and effective.

Sometimes a patient would say, "I can't," when, for example, discussing quitting smoking or letting go of an old anger. At those times, I found it helpful to point to a photograph on my wall, a souvenir of that night. It shows me walking through the fire. It is captioned, "If the impossible is possible then certainly the difficult is do-able."

Part II

Hypnosis

Chapter 3

Clinical Hypnosis

Hypnosis, and what we can do with it

Many of the case studies in this book center about the use of hypnosis. That being the case and because hypnosis is so poorly understood by both the lay public and much of the medical community, I want to give a brief overview here.

Hypnosis is one of our most ancient healing modalities, and one with an immensely long record of effectiveness; yet, like several other medical approaches, it has come into favor during some periods of history and has fallen from favor at other times. Other examples are herbal remedies, acupuncture, placebos, chemical treatment of emotional symptoms, and holistic therapy as examples of modalities that have been similarly acclaimed or disdained at various times and/or in various societies. Ancient though it is, hypnosis still is not universally accepted as an "orthodox" clinical method, but it is gaining more status.

In the ancient cradles of civilization, Persian magi and Greek oracles made use of hypnotic rituals and trances termed "temple sleep." Hypnotic methods were employed by Assyria-Babylonian physician-priests to exorcise and destroy demons held to be responsible for illness. As early as 500 B.C. the Egyptians utilized comparable techniques not only to appease their gods but to promote healing. In general, the ancient methods and hypnotic induction included deep, rhythmic breathing, repetitive prayers and chants, gazing, incense (to stimulate and focus the olfactory sense and establish a calm, receptive state), self-contemplation or yoga-like meditation. There was an array of rituals to engender the subject's concentration, cooperation, and expectation, the three key elements in establishing a state of hypnosis.

Modern hypnosis is generally considered to have been pioneered in 1889 by James Braid, an English physician. It was Braid who coined the term "hypnosis" from the Greek word *hypnos,* meaning sleep. This derivation, unfortunately, leads in large part to the misconception that hypnosis is some type of sleep state. A person in deep hypnosis is not asleep but merely in a state which superficially may resemble it.

In 1958 the American Medical Association recommended that all medical schools should include hypnosis training in their curricula.[3] This is a modality that not only has a wide range of psychotherapeutic uses (from recalling repressed memories to helping a patient program new behavior patterns) but can also affect physical responses. To understand some of the physical implications, consider this: if a person can gag, faint, or wince in pain as a result of what his or her mind perceives, then any illness involving blood flow or nerve impulse conduction can be treated at least in part by hypnosis.

Whether a person is sick or is enjoying good health sometimes depends on a precarious balance between disease fighting factors (immune response, medications, etc.) and disease causing factors (bacteria, viruses, faulty circulation, etc.). Visualize a balance scale with precisely ten pounds on one side delicately balancing ten pounds on the other side; the addition or subtraction of just an ounce one side would tip the scale. In therapy, the addition of hypnosis often can provide that small but effective weight shift.

Hypnosis to the therapist, however, is like the scalpel to the surgeon. I would no more advocate teaching hypnosis to a layman and saying, "Now that you can open a person's mind, you are a clinical hypnotherapist," than I would show that layman how to use a scalpel and say, "Now you are ready to go off and practice surgery." Neither would I advise with hypnosis taking the attitude of the proverbial little boy who having picked up a hammer sees everything in his world as a nail.

I used hypnosis extensively throughout my counseling practice. I hope the case studies in this book will help the reader better appreciate this ancient, still poorly understood and underutilized therapeutic tool.

Hypnosis is a difficult phenomenon to analyze. We have a

---

[3] William Kroger, *Hypnosis and Behavior Modification* , p. 9.

better grasp of what it is *not* than of what it *is.* Two common misconceptions are important to eliminate. Hypnosis is not sleep, nor is it a submissive trance in which a person's will is overcome by the will of the hypnotist. Even the experts cannot agree on a proper definition except to say that hypnosis is an altered state of awareness. Many will also stipulate that this awareness is often characterized by a heightened ability to concentrate. This description makes it clear that hypnoidal (hypnosis-like) states overtake our minds very often, although we do not recognize them as such.

Imagine a mother and her six-year-old son named Tommy, walking through a shopping mall. As the mother pauses to look into a shop window, the little boy lets go of her hand to pick up a toy he has dropped. For a fleeting moment the mother gets distracted. Then she looks down and the boy is gone, suddenly vanished among the crowd of shoppers. In that instant, she realizes Tommy is lost, and she begins frantically to look and listen for him.

If she hears someone call out another child's name, she may not even hear it. If her boy is wearing a yellow raincoat, she focuses on that color and may not see, almost certainly will not remember seeing, a boy of the same size passing by in a red raincoat. She need not *consciously* make a decision to watch for yellow and to hear certain sounds above all others; she automatically does so. She is listening for his voice, hoping to hear him call out, "Mommy!" And she is subconsciously hoping to hear someone who knows him call out his name. She is in an altered, heightened but narrowly focused state of awareness, alertness for the color yellow and the sound "Mommy" or "Tommy." This is a hypnoidal state which commonly occurs when we need to hone our attention.

People who feel light-headed or faint at the sight of blood have physiological reactions as if they themselves were bleeding. Likewise, gagging when you see someone vomit, or wincing when you see someone get hurt, is an example of hypnoidal responses in which your digestive or nervous system behaves as if you were injured. In clinical hypnosis, we simply help the patient to marshal and focus this natural ability toward a therapeutic goal.

As you read through some of my hypnosis cases you may see how I came to form my opinions regarding soul and spirit as part of each of us.

For purpose of confidentiality, except where otherwise noted, I have disguised the identities of the patients. In all other details, everything I relate will be factual. I have selected cases which I find to be typical or especially significant and verifiable. In some cases I will offer my assessments as well as alternative views. I do not have "the call of the missionary." I have drawn my conclusions, and I leave it to you to draw your own.

Part III

Case Studies

Regression Hypnotherapy

Chapter 4

The Night Screamer

Gertrude was a short, stocky, pleasant woman in her mid-fifties who came to me in the hope that hypnosis might help her stay with a diet and lose weight. She was my first paying patient for hypnosis therapy, and I was anxious to do especially well. It may be that I had another motive besides the wish to render effective treatment; I needed to prove to myself that I could use hypnosis beneficially. As I was later to see time and again in my practice, weight control is one of the most frustrating of common problems.

I performed a simple, standard induction and gave her post-hypnotic suggestions to the effect that she would enjoy the sensation of her hunger pains eating away her excess fat and want to prolong the sensation. When she was out of trance, I asked her how she felt.

"Well, I feel rested," she said. "It's a nice feeling. I don't get much rest."

She had not mentioned this previously. It occurred to me that she might have some problem more serious than an inability to stay on a diet and exercise. I asked her why she got so little rest.

"I don't sleep well," she said. "It's a wonder my husband has stayed with me all these years. I mean, I know I disturb him. I never sleep through the night. Two or three times a night I wake up, usually screaming. I've done it all my adult life."

"And you've never sought help for this?"

"No. what could anyone have done?"

I questioned her further, trying to help her pinpoint when this disruptive pattern began. She said that until she was about eighteen years old, she never had a problem sleeping. I asked her what had been going on in her life at that time.

"I got married when I was eighteen, and I became pregnant very soon."

Gertrude had already told me that she had no children. I asked her what had happened.

"It was terrible," she said. "I wanted that baby so much. We set up a nursery so our child would have a great start in life. We talked and planned for it. It meant a lot to us, especially to me. Then in the sixth month I just suddenly miscarried. It was horrible. I couldn't believe it. Every night for months I'd light a candle and go into the nursery. It sounds crazy but I wasn't just mourning. I think I was hoping to go in there and find a healthy baby in the crib. I never talked to anyone about it until now. I mean, it does sound crazy. If I still have nightmares, I don't remember them, but maybe that's why I wake up screaming. Do you think that could be it, Dr. Jarmon?"

"I'm sure it is, Gertrude," I said, knowing that with hypnosis it helps to sound positive. "You're a good hypnotic subject. Would you like me to regress you and end the night screams once and for all?

"My God, of course! Can you do that?"

Quickly I had her back in hypnotic trance, and I recounted to her the story she had just told me. But in doing so, while speaking to her subconscious mind, I brought the remembered episode to its conclusion with a healing affirmation. She had never fully come to closure of her tragedy, and she needed to embrace the loss and complete the final steps of the grief process.

"That life that once was growing inside you," I said, "was never born .There never was a baby in the nursery. The child never was born, never had to face the pains of this earthly existence and is at peace now. You and your husband have a good, loving life together even though you've had no children. Now your childbearing years are over and you're going on to the next chapters in life. There's no more need to wake up in the middle of the night. From now on, you'll sleep peacefully and soundly, and you'll wake up each morning refreshed." That entire procedure took no more than two minutes.

I confess that I was not totally certain of the outcome. After all, she was one of my first hypnosis patients, and my experience with it at that time was meager. But I was very careful not to betray my uncertainty. On the contrary, I knew I needed to instill trust. And to her surprise and delight (and mine), it worked.

After thirty-seven years of suffering, her problem was gone. That is, her night-screaming problem abruptly stopped. Weight control turned out to be much more difficult. I continued to see her for a year with the frustrating results that often accompany weight loss therapy. During that year, however, her nightly rest was peaceful and there was no recurrence of the terrified, screaming awakenings.

Then one day she called me to say that the screaming had come back. It happened right after she had undergone general anesthesia for a hysterectomy. She asked, "Do you think maybe the anesthesia wiped out the post-hypnotic suggestions you gave me and that doing the hypnosis over would again get rid of the problem?"

I assured her there was no "maybe" about it (why would I?), and immediately made an appointment for her. It required only one more brief hypnotic session to end her problem permanently. Her sleep disorder never returned.

Chapter 5

Claustrophobic Since Birth

"They are not sure I'm here"

Some people claim they can remember their own birth.

A person who retains that particular and astonishing image may THINK he actually remembers the birth, but perhaps he is only remembering descriptions of it from childhood which he later heard adults relate. On the other hand, I have seen cases that defy that easy explanation and can only be interpreted as individual's personal memories.

Roger was a tall, thin, clean-cut college freshman whose manner was lighthearted and relaxed. That is *usually*, but not always. His father had called me to make an appointment because of concern about his son's occasional, inexplicable bouts of claustrophobia. All his life, Roger had exhibited a mild fear, little more than nervousness, when confined in small, enclosed places. As he matured the fear had increased and now the claustrophobic episodes were becoming more frequent, yet, without any obvious pattern.

His fear seemed to be selective; that is, only certain types of enclosed situations troubled him. He could step into a small, but empty elevator or a walk-in closet without great trepidation. In contrast, he sometimes felt almost terrified in a crowded elevator, had difficulty making his way through any narrow passage between buildings, disliked riding in small cars, could not force himself to squeeze past throngs of people in a school corridor or airport, and felt a sensation of panic in narrow doorways or if people or objects pressed against him. Sometimes he even disliked being hugged.

During our first two sessions, Roger and I explored the nature of his problem but could not come to any conclusion about its cause. With the aid of hypnosis, I tried to provide him with some degree of desensitization and behavior modification, a conventional approach utilizing post-hypnotic suggestion. The results were unimpressive. We discussed if college life might in any way be exacerbating his problem. Perhaps subconsciously he felt daunted by college and had a sublimated impulse to quit, even though he was doing well both academically and socially. But that did not seem to be the problem, and that path of exploration led nowhere.

During our third session, I guided Roger into a deeper level of hypnotic trance, which was quite easy because he was a relaxed, cooperative subject. Rather quickly, he went into a deep hypnotic state, and I asked him to go back in his mind to where the problem first began. After a few moments of silence, he began to speak in a whispering but intense voice, obviously reliving an experience.

"Cramped-it's cramped. Walls... pushing in on me. I'm all hunched over ... can't get out, no place to go. I can see a little opening, a light. Water all around me ... The walls are pushing at me, pushing me toward the light. I want to kick. I'm kicking at it. I can't stand this pressure on me! There are people...people on the outside of where I am. They're afraid, too ..."

His face showed great anxiety. He hunched over in his chair with his arms crossed, up against his chest, his fists clenching and unclenching, his head lowered toward his knees, then he straightened somewhat and his legs kicked spasmodically. He was reliving some extremely traumatic experience and the fear that had accompanied it.

This is a startling but encouraging therapeutic sign. This abreaction, or delayed reaction, to a past, emotionally charged event can set the stage for a therapist's healing affirmation, which can enable the patient to relegate that event to its proper historical perspective. Roger had momentarily fallen silent, and I encouraged him to take up the account again.

"Go on. Tell it. Let it out. What happens now?"

"A gush of water... Something breaking through... It's over."

"Now what's happening?"

"Nothing." As Roger said that single word, "Nothing," his kicking stopped, he raised his head, and he leaned back in his chair, motionless and relaxed.

"Nothing? What do you see or feel now?"

"A baby. All I see is a baby lying there on a table. Not moving."

"Is the baby all right? Is it moving? Is the baby breathing?"

"No."

"Is there something more? What's happening now?

What do you see next?"

"I… I'm floating up… away from the baby. I'm going…into a tunnel of light."

By the time I worked with Roger I had treated some twenty patients who had undergone and recalled near-death experiences or NDEs, and Roger's was sounding very typical. Most of these survivors had recalled seeing a figure who spoke to them, directing them to return to their bodies, that is, to life. But so far, Roger had said nothing about such a figure or about being turned back.

"Do you see something or someone in the tunnel of light?", I asked.

"No. Nothing. Just the light, and down there the baby. A baby on a table."

I was perplexed, and a little uneasy. I could accept, even welcome, a patient's exhumed vision of a long forgotten birth trauma and near-death experience; because now it seemed that Roger had been reliving his own birth. But he was also re-experiencing his own soul's departure from the newborn infant's body; its departure without any turning back. If the soul had not returned, if it was not Roger's life force that returned, then who was this person in my office, reliving the throes of death? Perhaps the answer was that the baby, Roger himself, had not quite expired and had possessed such a strong will to live that it had returned of its own volition, without the need of being turned back from the tunnel of light.

"Look again, Roger," I urged him. "What now? What do you see next?"

"The baby. The baby is moving again. The baby is kicking and screaming… and a doctor is leaning over. More people… masks and caps… surgical gowns… people moving… baby moving…"

It was time to offer a healing affirmation. I told him that he had, indeed, seen a time in the past, the time of his birth, when a tightly enclosed space, the birth canal, had been a threat to his existence; but that whatever caused the problem, whatever the emergency had been, the experience had long ago and safely passed, and the cause of his fear was gone forever. There was no longer a need to be afraid of enclosed places.

Upon bringing him out of trance, I was mildly surprised to learn that he remembered nothing of what he had undergone only moments before; he recalled not a word of what he had said and not an inkling of what he had felt in trance. He asked what had happened, and I told him- in a general way, without dwelling on details, because I was not sure how he would react to it.

I was further surprised to find that he did not immediately grasp the significance of the scene he had revived: being hunched over, the walls pushing in on him, the water all around, and the opening of light. I had assumed that he would immediately realize he had re-experienced the view from the birth canal and a traumatic birth whose complications had almost brought him forth stillborn. But he did not.

"Well," l asked, "how do you feel?"

"Okay. A little strange, but okay."

"Roger, when you were born were there any complications?"

"Complications? No, none that I know of. Why?"

"Because that would explain what you just recalled in hypnosis. You seemed to be remembering your own birth. Don't you think so?"

"I was? I mean, I don't know. It sounds that way, doesn't it? But I don't know. If my Mom had a tough time delivering me, she never told me so. Dad didn't either. If that's so, they would have told me, or talked about it anyway, wouldn't they?"

"Well, maybe they thought it would bother you. No need to worry about it now. Let's get back to what's going on with you here and now. You're going back to school tonight, aren't you?"

He was, but would be on vacation at the end of the week. For the time being, at least, I decided not to tell him about his description of floating above the baby's body and going into the tunnel of light. He had enough to think about, and there was no need to dwell on anything other than the healing affirmation I had given him. I felt confident that he would now be able to conquer his claustrophobia. He should no longer have it because it was now an anachronism. It was no longer an appropriate reaction, like a uselessly repeated reflex long after the stimulus that triggered the reflex had stopped. We made an appointment for the following week. I told him to test for himself the healing process, to find out how well he was coming along by deliberately but safely putting himself into an environment that previously would have made him feel fearful.

"How do I do that?" he asked.

"Well, for instance, try walking through a narrow space between school buildings, or step into the school corridor between classes, or the entrance to the school cafeteria when it's mobbed at lunchtime. You don't have to put yourself through an ordeal. If you feel uncomfortable, just back out, and we'll try it again later. If you have any problems, call me. Otherwise, we'll get together next week and talk about your progress."

The following week, he arrived a little before his appointed time to tell me jubilantly that he had tested himself with complete success. In perfect comfort, he had tried everything I had suggested and had also stepped aboard a crowded elevator. "The only thing that bothered me was the heavy perfume the physics instructor wears. I don't know how her husband can stand it!"

We repeated the hypnotic regression and healing affirmations of the previous week, but I did not question him again about whether his mother had experienced great difficulty during his birth. If that were the case, evidently his family simply never mentioned it, and I doubted that he would ask them unless I told him to. I decided to drop the subject until I could discuss it with his parents.

A few days later, I called his mother to ask how Roger was doing. "Great!" she said. "Splendidly!" His claustrophobia simply seemed to have vanished.

Then I asked her if there had been any complications during his delivery.

"What?" she said in a startled voice. Then there was a long

pause. "Why, yes. Actually, there was. I went through a very long labor, and then, when the time came, I seemed to be delivering a stillborn baby. My water didn't break until almost the last minute, and nothing went right. He was limp and he couldn't breathe. The doctors tried hard to resuscitate him. I'd had a fairly normal pregnancy, and there weren't any signs of trouble until the time came, and then he just seemed to die before they could get him out.

They tried to get him breathing for a long time. I don't really know how long, and then they quit. The doctor told me it was all over. I was devastated. They put Roger off to the side in a crib and covered him with a sheet. Then while the doctor was trying to console me, a nurse saw the sheet move. She picked it up and Roger started screaming. It was incredible. They never found out what the problem was. Once he started breathing, he was perfectly all right.

But what a horrible scare we had. We asked the doctor if this would leave Roger with any lasting effects. He said only time would tell, and advised us to not say anything unless a problem came up. Telling him early on might give him unnecessary worry or even create a self-fulfilling prophesy of inadequacy. So we never told him about it. And thank God, he's never had any physical problems, just the ordinary things that kids get like colds and chicken pox.

But what in the world made you ask? Did my husband mention it? It's always been kind of a secret between us."

I told her, and she was astonished of course. She did not know what to make of my therapeutic procedure, but she and her husband were greatly relieved that their son's problem was finally gone. Naturally, Roger himself was even happier, and still is. The claustrophobic sensations have never returned. Soon after my conversation with his mother, she told him in detail about his difficult birth. He accepted that the memory of it must have lain dormant in his subconscious all these years, and he was glad to have had it brought forth and rendered harmless.

For my part, I always feel very good about such happy endings, but sometimes, I still wonder about his account of leaving his infant body, floating above the stillborn baby, seeing it, seeing the doctors work frantically over it, seeing it come alive again-yet without any memory of being turned back from the tunnel of light, without any memory of returning to his body. That was not like the other near-death experiences with which I had heard or read about. Had it truly been a near-death experience? Or is it possible that the soul of the fetus departed at birth, never turning back, and another soul, watching and ready, entered the lifeless infant, giving it life anew?

Chapter 6

The Woman Who Hated Money

"No Easy Pass for You Today"

It is our nature to try to avoid necessary pain. In fact, to seek out pain may be indicative of an emotional pathology. The well-integrated person only chooses pain in order to achieve a greater good such as studying late at night in order to do well on an examination, fighting hunger pains in order to lose fat, or straining at physical exercise in order to build up endurance and strength.

So patients strive to avoid unnecessary emotional pain when it comes to psychotherapy. As people heard of my work in past-life therapy, some hoped to see this as a relatively painless way to fix their emotional problems.

I advised patients that when the problems originate in this current life, it is this life's problems that need to be faced first. Attempts to side step the pain almost always end in frustration.

Such was the case with a woman I will call Alice. She presented an intriguing enigma: a professionally able and successful woman whose business was in constant danger of failure because she had tremendous difficulty in taking payments. She felt that accepting money for services was degrading and shameful, but did not know why.

Alice owned and ran a business providing social work and employee benefit consultation. She clearly knew that her service was skillful, caring, beneficial, and fully appreciated by her clients; yet, she felt extremely uncomfortable, almost humiliated, whenever the time came to accept fair payment for her work.

Many people in the care-giving professions have occasional qualms about this, but Alice's discomfort went far beyond that. It had always been a problem, but since she was seeing a therapist she kept holding onto a hope that the aversion would eventually dissipate. The last straw came, bringing her to tears one evening when she realized that without thinking she had thrown a large payment check into the wastebasket. She could not afford to throw away her livelihood.

Alice had heard about my work in past-life therapy, and hoped that this therapeutic modality might unlock a hidden cause of her problem. When her story unfolded, however, we discovered that in this case the causative trauma lay buried in the early years of her present life and not in a past incarnation.

In telling me of her past, she recounted a brutal childhood. Her mother had died three years ago and with that loss there began to flow a flood of emotions and memories from her early years. But by clouding over many other memories of those years, her mind had erected a defense against intense pain. She had always known that her formative years were spent in poverty. Several of her six siblings were struggling with their own emotional problems, but until relatively recently she had been unable to recall essentially any detailed childhood memories. Whole years were totally lost to her conscious awareness.

Then three years prior to our session she started to remember a horrific litany of emotional, physical, and sexual abuse perpetrated by her father who had died just as Alice was reaching puberty. But she still failed to discover the cause of her aversion to money, and she was hoping that PLT (past-life therapy) would uncover and fix the problem.

She proved to be a good subject and with use of standard hypnotic induction, I directed her to go back to where her problem about money originated. The following is a transcription of that session, lightly edited for clarity and confidentiality.

"Let's go back now to where the problem started," I said. "What's happening now?"

(No immediate response. The patient begins to weep.)

"It's all right," I said. "It's OK to cry, you can let it out."

''I'm inside." (Patient continues to weep.)

"Inside? Inside a house, a building? Is it cold? Hot?"

"It's warm." (Patient sobs.) ''I'm alone, all alone...''

"Now go to the next thing that happens. Can you see what you're wearing? Can you feel what you're wearing?"

"I'm little-I'm so little ". (more sobbing)

"Now what happens? Tell me the next thing that happens."

(No immediate response; more sobbing.)

"Now what happens? It's okay, it can't hurt you now. What do you see?"

(Long pause before the response.)

"She leaves ..."

"What do you mean, 'She leaves'? Did she leave her body? Did her soul leave her body? Was that not a good place to be?"

"She left her body."

"Why?" (Pause.) "Did she come to that body by mistake?"

"She doesn't want to be there. She didn't want to be born."

"Why? Why didn't she want to be born? Didn't she decide to come into that life?"

"They didn't want her." (Patient sobs again.)

"Did they try to abort her?"

(No response. Patient sobs and clutches at her right shoulder.)

"Now what happens?"

(Long pause.) "I have to come back again."

"Why? Why do you have to come back? "

"Everybody says I should *know* why. But I don't know why."

"It's okay. You'll remember and then you'll be able to feel better about it. You'll be more at peace."

"I need to love people. I need to ..."

"Go on. You're doing very well."

"I need to take care of Bill." (Bill, the patient's husband, had died after a lingering illness.)

"Tell me about the problem with money. Why is that? Why have you had trouble accepting it? Another scene is going to start to appear to you."

"It's...my mom's living room...and... he's there!"

"Who is?"

"My father."

"What's going on now?" (Patient resumes sobbing.)"About how old are you now?"

(Patient responds in a childlike voice.) "Five. I'm five years old."

"Is anybody else in the room? Now what happens?"

"He gives them something. He doesn't give me any...he doesn't give me any. I'm bad.." (Patient says loudly.) "I'm bad. I'm not good, I'm bad, I'm bad!" (Profuse sobbing.) "I'm bad . . . He never gives me anything because I'm bad. I tell. I tell!" (More sobbing.)

"You tell the truth. Does your father get mad when you speak the truth? Who tells you you're a bad girl?"

"He does. He yells at me."

"And then what happens?"

"My soul leaves my body ...I have to, I can't stand the pain ...I'm bad, too ...He couldn't buy me. He *couldn't* buy me. I'm strong ...I'm strong ..."

"You'll never let anybody buy you, will you?"

"No! Never ... Never . . . Never! Never!"

"When you see money coming at you ... "

"I don't *want* it! Get it away from me. Get it away...Get it away! I don't deserve it. I'm bad. I'm bad. I'm bad." (Patient again sobs profusely.)

"Time went on," I said comfortingly. "Time passed. Every day that went by, you became a day older. Every year that went by, you became a year older. One day he died, and he was never in that house to trouble you again. God has him now. Now he's the one who must look at all of the horrible things he did."

"I don't want him to hurt," Alice replied.

"He has to learn. We're all here to learn. He now knows the hurt, the pain he caused you. I want *you* to see that what he did resulted in money having a certain significance for you, a wrong, very wrong meaning. There are many who know you're a good person, and they want to give you money for your good services, and you'll accept that, because you *are* a good person. They have no ulterior motives; they aren't trying to bribe you, to buy your silence. They just know that fair is fair, and they want to give you money for an entirely different reason than your father wanted to. They give you money because they're grateful for the help you give them, not to buy them off."

As I spoke, I was gratified to see a peaceful expression return to Alice's face. Her body, which had sporadically become tense and rigid while re-experiencing her childhood defiance of her father's bribery, became totally relaxed. It seemed that he had bribed and threatened her brothers to keep them silent about his abuse. But he had failed to silence Alice. She had blotted out the memories of the abuse, the threats and attempted bribery, and the aftermath of additional pain when she refused the bribes and spoke the truth.

I continued with the healing affirmations and sensed that my words were having the desired effect.

"Alice, money now is one validation that you are a good and useful person. That's what money means now, that you have a worth. You are a worthy creature of God. Even the worst of us return to God, as your father has. When people give you money, that's just one way they are telling you they are grateful that God put you on this earth to help them, to provide good honest services for them. It's a validation. Be grateful that you have the ability to help people, and to earn money. There's nothing wrong with that, it's good. Now you'll see yourself doing a good job, doing it diligently, enjoying the fruits of your labor."

Watching her closely, I saw her relaxation expression turn to that of peace and contentment. Something about the lines of her mouth, her closed eyes, seemed to indicate a kind of satisfaction akin to pride. I knew our session was close to its successful conclusion as I continued.

"The worst parts of your life are over, long over. Your father can never harm you again. He regrets what he did, regrets it deeply. He knows he's going to have to come back and pay for that, and he will. But he knows, too, that you don't want to hurt him, you'd never hurt him, and you won't, ever. Now just rest, and heal in the light. Be at peace. Soon it will be time to fully resume your life, feeling wonderful about yourself and the good work you do."

Then I saw the gentle smile on her face that we had been working towards. I brought her out of hypnosis. The patient was surprised to realize that her money problem had stemmed from her father's abuse. She had thought that she had already successfully dealt with the traumatizing events of his mistreatment. Her near-death experience (NDE), was also a surprise.

Often, patients arrive with some concept of the causes underlying a problem and the concept may be correct, partially correct, or incorrect. In therapy I endeavored to keep all possibilities open so that the true origins of ongoing pain would not be bypassed or disguised. In this case, Alice discovered that her symptoms were produced by trauma in the childhood of her present lifetime, and it was more than enough trauma to account for a neurosis without any echoes emanating from a previous incarnation. She felt no compulsion to explore the possibility of past lives merely out of curiosity. She was happy to be healing and aware that just a little more therapy would probably be needed in order to definitively put her painful childhood behind her.

Chapter 7

Forgotten Injuries

To his neighbors and customers, Carl must have seemed a very normal, solid citizen, a healthy, reasonably content middle-class American of the twentieth century: forty years old, proprietor of a moderately prosperous hardware store. He was a happily married father of four. He was clean-shaven, dressed casually, but neatly, of medium height and build, with a slightly ruddy complexion and sandy colored hair almost hiding a few early wisps of gray. He smiled easily and expressed himself with confidence in a firm, rather deep baritone voice.

There would have been no reason to notice him in a crowd. But anyone who spent much time with him would sooner or later see that something was not quite right. Beneath his normal, healthy appearance, evidently maintained by rigorous self-control, there was a restless mass of fears and idiosyncrasies that occasionally burst through his calm outward manner during moments of stress. When nervous, he trembled, sometimes flailed his limbs, and felt his throat constrict as if he were choking. Any small change in the course of his life was more distressing to him than it would be to an emotionally healthy person.

He sought therapy to obliterate these symptoms and find the cause of his vague feelings of anxiety and depression. An excellent hypnotic subject, he was able to go into deep trance early in our work, and under hypnosis he began to uncover incidents of childhood abuse -- physical, emotional, and sexual, of which he had not been consciously aware. He also revealed several past-life scenarios which seemed to explain some of his fears and reactions to stress, particularly the choking and limb flailing. These sessions of hypnotic regression had a clearly cathartic effect. He would envision a past-life experience of being hung that triggered those reactions, and I would then give him an appropriate healing affirmation before bringing him out of hypnosis.

Afterward, there was no recurrence of his nervous symptoms, and I was satisfied that his therapy was progressing well. All the same, I sensed, as did Carl, that at least two other still shrouded aspects of his past remained somehow to be resolved. One of these involved his wife, who was a positive factor in his life. He had shared a past life existence with her, and now he had a strong sense that he had come into his present existence, in his words, to "help her with something she needs to do in this life."

Hypnotic regression is a marvelously revealing tool of therapy but carries no implication of omniscience. Carl and I never did discover precisely what his wife needs to do in this life that requires his help. Perhaps what she and he needs is simply the close bonding and mutual support of their good marriage. Carl's wife has no idea what the "something" might be, and no urgency to discover it. If her future holds some ordeal, effort, or accomplishment demanding his help, she knows he will be there. He knows it, too, and that is enough.

But what about that second, still shrouded aspect of his past? Although I could not guess what it might be, and had no way of knowing whether it had occurred in his current life or in a previous existence, I felt certain that his subconscious held some memory that needed to be addressed.

When therapy is going well (and sometimes when it is not), a rapport grows between therapist and patient. The psychiatrist may detect, or merely suspect, some hidden, unresolved problem, although the stimulus or clue that prompts the suspicion is not always readily apparent. The clue, in fact, may be nothing more definite than a fleeting expression on the face of the patient, a gesture, a manner of speaking, a mild feeling of malaise, or a tendency to make cryptic or seemingly irrelevant remarks. In Carl's case, I tried without success to analyze what clues he might have given me, but I was not surprised when one day he came to his session looking distraught.

At first he volunteered no reason for his obvious distress, but upon questioning, he said that for several days he had been having terrible headaches and severe abdominal pain. I began to question him further on the assumption that I might have to refer him to another doctor for treatment of a physical ailment. Then he said that what bothered him even more than his pain was a deep sense that something was about to come out of him, as if he needed to regurgitate something. He had no conscious awareness of what the something might be, and his sense of it was mental rather than physical, involving no feeling of nausea or convulsion.

Then he became somewhat more talkative than usual. He said he had been thinking a lot lately about an only vaguely remembered incident that had occurred when he was eleven years old. While riding his bicycle, he had fallen hard and fractured his skull. He did not know why he had been recalling and rethinking about that accident lately, except that his headaches perhaps brought back the memory of the pain of that skull fracture. Then I remembered a comment in our last session.

While under hypnosis during previous sessions, he had recalled that fall, but the way he remembered it, he had hit the street and then been aware only of standing somewhere looking down a steep stairway, like a sudden change of scene in a movie.

There were no more details. Maybe in peeling the proverbial psychological onion, we were now close enough to find what that elusive problem was. Under hypnosis, I asked him to go back to that day when his skull was fractured. The following story came out.

Once again he was a boy of eleven, and he was riding his bike to a friend's house. He was pedaling fast when the front wheel hit something and turned sharply sideward. He felt himself hurtling through the air, and then he hit the street, hard. He stood up, shaken, bruised, lacerated, and scared, but his head had not struck the pavement! The bruises and scrapes were painful, however, and he decided to turn back and walk his bicycle home.

When he arrived, he called out to his mother, but heard no response and could not find her downstairs. He went up to her bedroom and heard her inside, talking softly. He opened the bedroom door and walked into the room. She was in bed with a man, not his father but a stranger. Leaping from the bed, the man shouted, "Don't you knock before you come in?"

Thoroughly startled and confused, Carl took several steps backwards, but the man lunged forward. Just as the boy turned around to run downstairs, the man struck his back, pushing him hard. Carl toppled down the steep stairway, hitting his head on the floor below.

Now, almost thirty years later, Carl was reliving the experience under hypnosis, vividly seeing the enraged man pursuing him even after he had fallen. "He's after me," Carl said breathlessly. "He's coming down and I can't move. I can't get away. He's going to kick me. He's kicking me in the stomach, and I can't move!"

I asked him what happened next. Clutching his abdomen and grimacing, he replied, "He's kicking my stomach."

Then, quite abruptly, the expression of pain and fear left Carl's face. "Now I'm going into the light," he said. "It's so peaceful. I see some people. I don't know who they are. It's too bright to make out their faces. I want to stay here. Now I see a kind, older man. He appears and puts his hand on my shoulder. He says I'll have to go back. I tell him I don't want to. He says, 'I know you don't want to, but there's someone you're going to meet who needs you. You'll be all right. You'll make it.'"

I said nothing for a few moments, waiting to see if Carl would continue, but he sat there silently. Finally, I asked him what happened next. His only response was to clutch his abdomen, writhe in pain, and begin weeping. He had gone through enough, and I decided to give him a healing affirmation without further delay. I assured him that he had done the right thing, the only thing he could do, and I reaffirmed that everything would work out happily, as it was meant to. Bringing him back to the present, I told him gently that the attack, the injuries to his head and stomach, the pain were now many years behind him and, having brought the long-blocked memory forth at last, he would no longer be troubled by headaches and abdominal pain.

His conscious mind had been unable to face the memories of all that had happened *after* his minor bicycle accident, the discovery of his mother with a lover, the vicious attack by the lover, the fall downstairs, the skull fracture when he hit the floor below, the terrible kicks to his abdomen, even his subsequent treatment at a hospital where he had come so close to death. He saw himself going over to the other side, "into the light," only to be turned back, because it was not yet his time to die.

Other patients have told me of near-death experiences and their accounts have been eerily similar, all of them agreeing about a sensation of light, or going up and into a place or tunnel of light, and some of them seeing people (or spirits? Or angels?) waiting to greet them or turn them back to continue on with their lives.

Unable to bear those terrible memories, Carl had totally blocked them out of his consciousness, retaining only the memory of the fractured skull and even altering that memory, blending it and attributing it to, his fall from the bicycle.

Carl would understand that, "there's someone you're going to meet who needs you." That person was, of course, his future wife, and for that matter the fruit of their union, their children. That single hypnotic session had uncovered curative insights for the patient.

It was time to bring Carl out of trance, and I did so after first directing him to visualize a resting place of peace and light. I asked him how he felt.

"Tired," he said, "but okay. The headache's gone. The stomach pain, too."

He was perspiring a little, and he wiped his face and nose with his handkerchief. As he did I noticed something I had never before seen in patients after hypnotic regression.

"Carl," I said, "do you now remember everything that happened that day?"

"Yes, I think so," he said. "Everything is clear now."

"Well, do you happen to remember, with everything that happened when you got home and the stranger attacked you, when you fell downstairs, did you get a bloody nose?"

"Yes, come to think of it," he said. "Why do you ask?"

I pointed to his handkerchief. It was splattered with blood.

Past Life Therapy - PLT

Chapter 8

Terror and Seizures at the Full Moon

George was a well-dressed, well-mannered, well-spoken forty-two-year old businessman, highly regarded in his community. His wife, Maria, brought him into my office in the hope that I could do something about "George's period", a term they both used to describe what had been happening with George once a month for more than twenty years. At the time of the full moon, George would become inexplicably agitated. Sometimes, in fact, this calm, friendly gentleman became a frightened, hostile mass of irrational energy. At such times, he seemed to feel that, wherever he was, he was in danger and must flee. If asked where he would go, he had no idea, and did not care. He just felt the compulsion to escape.

His symptoms had first begun to appear at about the age of twenty. At that time he also spontaneously developed a seizure disorder, to which his monthly bouts of paranoia might or might not be related. CAT scans and electroencephalograms had revealed an area of scarring in the left temporal region of his brain, the cause for which was never determined. The seizures had been controlled with Tegretol and phenobarbital, and the patient was still taking the latter medication when he came to see me. The periodic paranoid behavior had never been addressed.

Maria persuaded him to seek my help because his intense emotional episodes were taking a severe toll on her own mental health. During several of his recent "periods" he had been ready to abandon everything: his wife, his home, his career. He just "had to get away fast," as he told me, and added that he felt he would die if he did not flee.

He and Maria had been married about two years when she realized that his paranoid behavior always occurred at the time of the full moon. When I was a senior student at New Jersey Medical College, I wrote a research paper on the statistical relationship between certain environmental and atmospheric factors and crimes of passion in the City of Newark. One of the factors with a high degree of correlation to certain crimes was the full phase of the moon,[4] a phenomenon familiar to the police. I did not have the opportunity to explore the possible causative influences, and after my research was presented and published I pursued the subject no further as I had to get on with the rest of my medical training. I never expected that decades later I would be addressing the subject again.

During his first office visit, George was the picture of composure, an affable, fluent conversationalist with a ready smile. Many people, including psychotics, can make a good impression even while disturbed, still the accounts of his behavior during the full moon were hard to imagine.

We proceeded with a standard psychiatric interview, and nothing emerged which might account for the bizarre behavior described. Our second and third sessions went much the same way. Our fourth session was scheduled to coincide with the full moon, and I hoped I might then gain a better sense of what I was dealing with. I was not disappointed.

George and Maria arrived in separate cars. He was markedly agitated. He could hardly sit in his chair. His eyes darted about the room as if he were expecting that at any moment he would be caught by an unseen enemy.

He said, in a somewhat aggressive tone, that he had insisted on driving his car to my office because he intended to leave Maria as soon as the session was over. When I asked him precisely what he intended to do, he said he would just get into his car and leave as fast as he could. He intended to abandon his job, possessions, everything. Fear and bewilderment clearly showed through the bravado. He could offer no explanation save that he just had to get away.

I was able to persuade him to do some deep breathing and guided imagery exercises, calming him down and taking him into

---

[4] Harold Feldman, M.D., and Robert G. Jarmon, M.D., "Factors Influencing Criminal Behavior in Newark: A Local Study in Forensic Psychiatry," *Journal of Forensic Sciences,* Vol. 24, 1979.

a relaxed state, but it took some time. That was as far as I got. I had not yet begun hypnosis when my next patient arrived. I had to end the session, but at least I had glimpsed the behavior that had brought him there.

Evidently, his state of tormented agitation soon subsided, for he did not leave his wife and he showed up the following week for another scheduled session. Having felt somewhat uneasy about ending the previous session without rendering much help, I was relieved to see him. The full moon was waning and so were his apprehensions. Early during his fifth visit, I took him into a hypnotic state. He proved to be an excellent subject going into trance deeply. Perhaps now some progress could be made.

I directed him to go back in time to when his anxiety about the full moon started. He unhesitatingly related how as a teenager, while he was working at a summer job on a moonlit night, three friends had stopped by and invited him to join them. He could not get off duty. The friends went on without him. They died that night in a freak automobile accident.

He told the story with little display of emotion, but I thought perhaps we had found the root of his anxieties. I gave him the sort of healing affirmation previously described in this book assuring him that the death of his friends was not his fault, that he himself had been very fortunate that night, and that he no longer had any cause to feel anxiety on nights of the full moon. He did not respond with an expression of understanding or peace as I had hoped and expected. Instead, he spontaneously seemed to slip into a deeper trance. Now he became emotional, fearful.

He spoke in broken sentences about soldiers, enemy lines, and bombings. I did not get a clear picture of what he was relating, but I felt that whatever it was, he had expended enough emotional energy for the time being. Again, I gave him a healing affirmation followed by a post-hypnotic suggestion that the next time he went back to that scene he would see it clearly.

On coming out of trance, he remembered little of what he had said, so I described what he had revealed about the memory of the night when his friends were killed in the auto accident. It was no surprise to him; he had always consciously remembered the tragedy. But he did not remember anything related to the other experience he had visualized. When I asked him about his vision of soldiers in wartime, he had no explanation.

His wife then told me something she felt might have a bearing on this image of war. Once, when George was suffering through his full-moon paranoia, he became so uncontrollable that she called the police. When they arrived, George ran into the bathroom and cowered under the sink. Judging by what he said, he must have thought the two uniformed men were German soldiers, and speaking German (a language he does not know), he begged them not to shoot him. The police later remarked to Maria that this was not the first time someone had reacted to their arrival in such a strange manner. Perhaps they were merely trying to comfort her or perhaps such occurrences are not uncommon. In any event, no one knew what to make of it. George's next office visit proved to be the most startling of all. He went into trance rapidly and deeply, and he immediately became visibly apprehensive.

"They're going to get me tonight," he exclaimed in a hoarse whisper. "I know it. They'll spot me! I told command we couldn't go ahead with the mission on a night like this. Look at that moon. My God, you could read a newspaper in this light. They'd have to be blind not to get me."

"Who's going to get you?" I asked.

"The Germans! They'll spot us, for God's sake. I told command it couldn't be done...not to make me do it tonight; but they wouldn't listen. They said it had to be done. I believed all that talk about going home. FDR said we'd be home for Christmas, didn't he? It's almost Thanksgiving, and it looks like I'll never see home."

"Where is home?" I asked.

He gave me the name that could be that of a town and said it was in Missouri.

I did not know how much was fantasy or reality, but I had a strong feeling that this story line was the path my patient needed to take. I asked him other details of his life: what his name was, where and when he had gone to school, where he had worked, who were the members of his family. He answered all my questions without hesitation.

Then, slipping back into the war scene, he said he was an American officer, assigned to operate clandestinely behind enemy lines during World War II, to help refugees sneak through German lines to the West. The rest of the story was brief and came quickly.

One night, in a small town under the bright light of the full moon, he was spotted by a German sentry. The exchange of a few words was sufficient for the sentry to realize he was a foreigner. The sentry shouted for help and more German soldiers raced forward. They had no intention of bringing him back to their commanding officer. They knew he was a spy or saboteur, and that was all they wanted to know. They forced him down to a river bank. The light of the full moon was shining off the water and into his face when they shot him in the back and in the left side of his head.

"I'm shot," he said. "My back. My head." Then he was silent.

"And now," I asked, "is there more? What happens now?"

"I'm floating into a tunnel of light. There's Joe. Joe went through basic training with me. I haven't seen him since. I guess Joe didn't make it either."

Then he said he saw his mother and father who had died when he was young. After that, he was silent again. It was time to give the patient a healing affirmation. I assured him that he had been right to fear the full moon on that terrible night of war. Its brightness did give his position away and he was caught, killed; but the war was over now, long over; he was back in America, his soul now occupied a new body. He no longer had cause to be terrified of the full moon.

When I brought him out of trance, he looked weary but said he felt strangely light and peaceful. He was not aware of the vast majority of what he had said, so I told him the story in full, as he had told it to me. He was understandably puzzled, but not in an unpleasant way. Again he remarked that he felt light, peaceful, and added only that he needed to think about all this.

After that session, he reported that his symptoms of paranoia during the full moon had almost entirely disappeared. The inexplicable sense of foreboding was nearly gone. We conducted two more such sessions and his symptoms totally left.

Out of curiosity, his wife told me that she looked for and found that small town in Missouri in an Atlas and contacted the high school there. She told the school secretary she was trying to trace the whereabouts of a relative. The secretary looked in the school records for the name the soldier had used and said, "Yes, he graduated here, but a year earlier than you said, but that must be him, all right."

I ordered two subsequent electroencephalograms for George. Neither showed the signs of scarring in the left temporal lobe and there was no seizure-like activity. Sometimes EEGs can spontaneously revert to normal. A curious occurrence took place during the second of these tests. We were using a halter, portable twenty-four hour EEG. I had wanted a halter EEG so that I could record his brain-wave patterns during hypnosis as he experienced his past life as a soldier, his death at the hands of enemy soldiers, and while going into the tunnel of light.

I asked a colleague of mine to analyze the EEG tracings. At the time he was an examiner for the National Board of Neurology and Psychiatry, testing neurologists and psychiatrists on their ability to interpret EEGs. He told me that the brain wave pattern generated when the patient was going into the "tunnel of light" was that of a person in deep sleep, not hypnosis. But my patient was not asleep, he was talking, as demonstrated on the videotape that I made of the session. I asked the neurologist if this could be the pattern of a person talking in his sleep and he said, "No."

Clearly more research needs to be done in this area of near death experiences incorporating the use of EEGs.

That night, while still wired to the EEG recorder, George lay down on his living room sofa to take a nap. He was awakened suddenly by his dog madly barking at someone standing at the end of the sofa. It was not Maria; she had gone up to bed. George looked up and saw to his amazement his old girlfriend, Inga, from Missouri, from his previous life. Dumbfounded, he stammered, "What are you doing here?"

There was no reply. She gazed at him for a moment and then faded away, and the dog stopped barking.

When George told is wife what had happened, she actually got angry at him for seeing an old girlfriend behind her back.

Sometimes a guy just can't win.

We stayed in contact for four years. His twenty year history of monthly psychotic episodes was over. Gradually, he ended his use of anti-seizure medication and had no further seizures as of my last follow up.

George had told me that although the experience of seeing Inga was incredibly real, he tried at first to tell himself it was merely the result of awakening suddenly from a vivid dream. But then he realized that the vision had not appeared to him alone. His dog had seen her first and had awakened George with his barking.

****

Can you imagine the problematic discussion with his insurance carrier if I tried to explain that the cause of the patient's temporal lobe epilepsy and concomitant paranoia was secondary to a gunshot wound to his head in a previous life? After denying the claim due to a <u>pre-existing condition</u> ("The injury has to at least have happen in this lifetime, doctor!") and recommending I refer it to the V.A., they would undoubtedly drop my name from their list of approved therapists.

Chapter 9

When Anna was Elizabeth

Until 1986, the concept of reincarnation held no interest for me. I considered it the stuff of fiction, supermarket tabloids, and exotic or primitive religions with no more reality (or relevance in my life) than a belief in leprechauns. Then, in the spring of that year, I received a phone call from a woman whom I will call Anna. She told me she was a nurse, and she had found my name in the yellow pages of the phone directory. She wanted to begin a weight-reduction program.

I wondered why a practicing nurse would look for a therapist in the phone directory instead of asking a doctor for a referral, and it was not even her own county's directory for she lived some distance from me. I wondered if she had some other problem beyond a need to diet and exercise. I had no idea that my subsequent encounters with Anna would change my beliefs, my clinical approach and convictions, my life. When she arrived at my office for our first session, there seemed nothing unusual about this somewhat overweight but pleasant-looking woman in her mid-thirties who was concerned about her physical fitness and appearance.

Having used hypnosis successfully and often to alter undesirable habit patterns, I used it again in this instance to help Anna lose weight. She proved to be an excellent subject. The results were encouraging. Over the next two months, she showed considerable progress toward her goal. But then, quite suddenly and unexpectedly, she developed right-lower-quadrant abdominal pain and tenderness, and her menses stopped. She asked me if hypnosis could alleviate these symptoms, but I was concerned about what was *causing* the symptoms. Having worked in emergency medicine for many years, I had occasion to deal with hundreds of cases of abdominal pain. She could be suffering from an ovarian cyst, colitis, diverticulitis, appendicitis, or perhaps an ectopic pregnancy wherein the fetus develops not in the uterus but in a Fallopian tube or in the peritoneal cavity.

Although she said she was having an active sex life, she dismissed any possibility of pregnancy. Supposedly "impossible" pregnancies occur rather often, however, and I was not about to take chances with the patient's life.

I immediately started a diagnostic workup, but the pregnancy test was negative, and the complete blood count (CBC), urinalysis, and electrolytes proved unremarkable. Her symptoms were steadily intensifying; her abdomen was becoming more swollen and tender, and she was getting weaker. Although I insisted that she see her gynecologist immediately, she at first refused, declaring that nothing very serious could be wrong.

Two weeks later, I repeated the blood studies at a different lab, but the results were the same, nothing abnormal. All the while she was becoming weaker and more pain ridden. I became adamant and told her I would not make another appointment with her until she obtained a thorough gynecological evaluation. Reluctantly, she agreed.

On the basis of a first, thorough examination, her gynecologist made a presumptive diagnosis of ectopic pregnancy and notified the operating room. While the O.R. was being readied for an emergency laparotomy (exploratory abdominal surgery) the doctor sent her to the sonography lab. Fifteen minutes later, the sonography technician called the doctor to tell him no ectopic pregnancy or other masses showed on the sonogram. The operation was canceled, and he sent her back to me. Thanks a lot!

In psychiatry there is a condition known as conversion disorder, also called hysterical neurosis. In it a person may have what appears to be a physical condition such as blindness or paralysis, which has no physiologic basis. Pseudocyesis, or false pregnancy, is one such condition. With it a woman may experience all the signs of pregnancy including weight gain, nausea, and amenorrhea without being pregnant. My first thought was that Anna's condition might be a form of that.

Her symptoms continued. During one of her subsequent sessions with me and five months to the day after her last menstrual flow, Anna was telling me about her mounting though vague, nonspecific feelings of anxiety and depression. Apart from her weight and her distressing abdominal symptoms, she seemed to have some personal problem which she could not or would not verbalize. I put her under hypnosis and instructed her, "Go back now to where your problem started. Go back to where it began."

I was in no way prepared for what was to follow. In deep trance, she held her right side and began to moan as I questioned her. "Tell me what's happening to you," I said. "What's troubling you, and where and when is this happening."

"Long ago." She replied, "Long ago, not now, not here."

"Where, Anna? When"?

"My name is Elizabeth," she replied, and then her story unfolded.

She spoke of what sounded like a different lifetime in which she was Elizabeth, nineteen years old, and in her fifth month of pregnancy. She was in Europe but she did not say precisely where. She seemed to regard my questions about that as odd, as if I should know something so obvious. As to when, it was centuries ago, but again she was not specific. Her reaction was as if the question was irrelevant, the answer obvious, and her need to recall the scene itself far more important. Her pregnancy had become very difficult, continually painful, and now a priest and a physician were at her bedside. She could hear them talking.

"We must take the baby," the physician said. "We must take it from her or the woman will die."

"No!" the priest said emphatically. "We cannot take life even to save a life. You will not kill the unborn infant. If God wills that the woman die, then she dies."

With that, Anna became visibly weaker, and then a look of peacefulness came over her face. Suddenly, she became absolutely still. It as if her heart and breathing had stopped. I checked for and was relieved to find a pulse.

"Anna," I said quickly, "what is it? What's happening?"

When she did not answer, I realized my mistake. *"Elizabeth,"* I said to her, "you must tell me what's happening."

"I've died. I'm floating now. I'm floating up-into a tunnel of light." I had counseled several patients who had undergone near-death experiences, and her account sounded startlingly like theirs, the floating and rising up into a tunnel or source of light. I suddenly had a very chilling thought, what if this patient goes into this light of death and is not turned back? All of my other patients had their NDEs in this lifetime. This patient was experiencing dying centuries ago. Could this kill her?

I talked to her soothingly, giving her a healing affirmation that the pain of her previous life in a different body, had died when that body died and would no longer afflict her. This was therapy on the fly. Then I rapidly brought her out of trance.

"My God, you finally did it, Dr. Jarmon. I feel great. The pain is gone!" So was her abdominal swelling, tenderness, and generalized weakness. She had no recollection of what she had said during trance.

Afterward I sat alone in my office thinking about what I had heard and seen and trying to understand it. At the same time I felt the excitement of discovery. The marvel of it was not over, as I discovered that evening. She phoned me that night very happy and relieved to say that her menstrual flow had returned. I did not know what to make of this and hardly knew what to say. All I could think of in response was to reschedule her next visit for the following week and tell her I was glad for her.

During that next visit, I put her into deep trance and regressed her back to that deathbed scene. Very quickly she went into an even deeper trance and right back to there. When she spoke this time, she addressed me as if I were the priest at her bedside.

I decided to play the role of the priest and see where this experience of a previous life would lead. "Elizabeth," I said, "do you understand that God forbids the taking of life? Do you understand why I cannot permit the physician to kill the infant by taking it from you?"

"Yes, Father," she replied.

"Do you have anything you wish to tell me, Elizabeth?"

"No, Father, I have confessed my sins. I am ready to die."

I hesitated. I had no idea what to say next. As we sat there while I was thinking about where to take this, she spoke and broke the silence.

"Oh, my God," she intoned, "I am heartily sorry..."

"Elizabeth," I said. "Elizabeth? Anna?"

"...for having offended thee," she continued, "and I detest all my sins because I dread the loss of heaven and the pains of hell, but most of all..."

I did not interrupt her again. Her prayer was very familiar to me as a Catholic. I was astonished.

"...because they have offended Thee, my God, who art all good and deserving of my love..."

She was reciting the Act of Contrition, the prayer a Catholic says at the end of confession or during last rites.

But Anna is Jewish, as are her parents, her husband, and her entire family. After bringing her out of trance, I asked her about it.

"Anna, do you know the Act of Contrition?"

"Act of Contrition? No, what kind of act is it?"

I repeated it for her and then asked, "Anna, does it sound familiar to you? It's a Christian prayer."

"No," she said, "I've never heard it before. I'm Jewish, you know."

"Yes, I know," was all I could think to say to her. What I said to myself, however, was, "I have a feeling, Bob, we have just begun a journey unlike any we could ever dream up. Hang on tightly for what could be a wild ride."

Chapter 10

A Reunion of Ancient Colleagues

I was amazed Anna's ability to recite a prayer she had never heard in her present life, but it was far from the last surprise.

She lost the weight she wanted to lose during the course of our counseling sessions, and her regression to a previous life as Elizabeth ended all symptoms of ectopic pregnancy. Her depression and ill-defined anxieties also lifted. Some current issues still troubled her, so we continued therapy. During subsequent hypnotic session she described ten more lifetimes.

I still did not know what to make of this, and wondered if I might be dealing with a multiple-personality disorder, or even simple confabulation. I did not know then that what I was doing was past-life therapy and that I was not the only practitioner. I was also not aware that relationships between souls can carry over from one life to another with different relationship dynamics.

Anna had experienced some lifetimes that were happier or easier than others, and she actually had a favorite. In that life, she had worked in what she described as a "healing temple", and she was quick to add that I had worked there, too. She said the temple was adorned with a symbol, a butterfly, and behind the pillared building was a garden with an adjacent pool where the healers went to refresh themselves at the end of the day and have a cup of wine.

I was still not sure what to make of all of this, but the concept of transference was always in my mind. Transference is a relationship whereby a patient transfers onto the therapist the feelings he or she had for an earlier authority figure.

Her description of the temple intrigued me. My office was in my home, which had large pillars at the front. More perplexing was her mention of the garden and pool behind the temple. Behind my home, I have a garden and adjacent pool, but she had never seen them and could not have known about them. Neither could she know about a small glass pane with a butterfly etched into it over my backdoor. She could not identify the time or place of this healing temple (though she was certain she had been there many centuries ago), so there was no way I could try to verify much of what she related. Absent any corroborating it all sounded like it would remain nothing more than a fanciful scene. I told none of my colleagues about this unusual case.

Several months later, while in my local bookstore picking up a book which had been suggested to me by my next past-life patient, I noticed a book lying atop others on a shelf. Out of curiosity, I took it down. It was entitled *Many Lives, Many Masters,* by Brian L. Weiss, M.D. The phrase "many lives" caught my attention, and since the author was a doctor, I was curious enough to read the jacket copy on the book: "The true story of a prominent psychiatrist, his young patient, and the past-life therapy that changed their lives." Dr. Weiss was head of the psychiatry department at Mount Sinai Hospital in Miami. I bought the book, and what I read astounded me.

Dr. Weiss and I shared identical experiences and reactions to the accounts of patients under deep trance. The coincidences, if that's what they were, did not end there. Our fathers had the same names, the same religion, the same age and time of death, and the same mode of death. They also both worked for a time at Fort Monmouth. Brian's father was a photographer and my father was a medical administrative officer. I have photos of my father which were taken by Brian's. Our mothers-in-law had died of the same disease while we had helped them as well as we could to "pass over" into death. We are the same age and horoscope sign. We had never known each other, but we had grown up only five miles apart.

His book is an account of his therapy sessions with a patient named Catherine (a pseudonym to protect her confidentiality) who, like my patient, Anna, worked in a hospital. In deep hypnosis, Catherine also recalled past lives. Eventually, in fact, she dumfounded Dr. Weiss by claiming to have had eighty-six previous lives and by actually recalling, describing in some detail, a full dozen.

Catherine had sought psychiatric therapy because she had been suffering from deepening depression, anxieties, and phobias.

Once, when she was very young, she had been pushed into a swimming pool, but that episode did not seem to explain her irrational fear of drowning. The reason for this particular phobia became clear as she recalled one of her previous lives, which had ended with drowning. Similarly, much of her depression and recurrent anxieties could be interpreted in the light of her previous incarnations. In one life, she had been among the thousands of victims of an epidemic; in others, she had experienced abuse, lifelong poverty, and incidents of fear or mistreatment. As Dr. Weiss pointed out, such traumatic experiences, even the less severe ones, affect our mental health and ability to function and get ground into our psyches.

But Catherine's mental health improved dramatically as she recalled both the serene and horribly traumatic experiences her soul had undergone in past incarnations. The process seemed to purge her present-life psyche of accumulated burdens. In dealing with Anna, I was beginning to speculate that the modern perception of death is not real; that death is not obliteration for all eternity; that the soul survives; and that the realization of this survival could have great therapeutic value.

In the eighth chapter of his book, Dr. Weiss summarized some of his basic conclusions about the type of therapy, and I found myself in total agreement with those conclusions. He pointed out that Catherine's improvement was dramatically rapid without the aid of any medication. He ascribed the therapeutic progress to "a force apparently much more effective than conventional therapy or modern medicines." This "force," he explained, included remembering and sometimes actually reliving not only severe, dramatic traumas but also the "daily insults to our bodies, minds, and egos", the unhappiness and misfortunes that in greater or lesser degree assault all human beings.

As he scanned Catherine's previous lifetimes and gently probed them with his questions, he had sought the patterns of those insults to the mind and emotions, just as a psychiatrist practicing more conventional therapy seeks patterns while listening to a patient's account of traumatic events and reactions to those events. "The technique," he explains "was similar to reviewing a childhood in conventional therapy, except that the time frame was several *thousand* years, rather than the usual ten or fifteen years."

My own experiences and conclusions were precisely paralleling Dr. Weiss'. In fact, they were identical as if we both trained together. But long before I reached the eighth chapter, where he presents his conclusions, on page sixty-four in Chapter Five, I read something more astonishing. At this point, Catherine had been reviewing a lifetime in which she had pierced her foot with some sharp object and had gone to a healing temple to have the resulting infection treated. She went on to describe a bleak and poverty-stricken life in which she aged rapidly and soon died. The vivid recollections seemed to exhaust her, and Dr. Weiss decided to bring her out of hypnosis quickly.

Before he could do so, however, she suddenly declared that someone named Robert Jarrod needed his help. He had no idea who Robert Jarrod might be, and during a subsequent hypnotic session he questioned her about her strange, unexpected statement.

When he asked her who Robert Jarrod was, she replied, "I don't know ...He may be in another plane, not this one." By this she meant that Robert Jarrod might not be in the lifetime or period between lives which she was then recalling. Catherine added, "Only when he wants, only if he decides to come to me, he will send me a message. He needs your help."[5]

As I read the passage I was thunderstruck. The mounting coincidences were too many and too great to *be* coincidences. Dr. Weiss had understood Catherine to say "Robert Jarrod", and perhaps she had but I wondered if she was saying "Robert Jarmon". I wrote to Dr. Weiss that evening. When he received the letter, he phoned me. Even before he read it, he knew. He said that when he saw my name over the return address on the envelope, he realized that Jarmon was the name his patient was trying to say.

Thus began a series of letters and phone calls. He was planning to come from Florida for a lecture, and we arranged to

---

[5] Brian Weiss, *Many Lives, Many Masters,* p. 64.

meet in New York City. Shortly before the meeting took place, I had a session with Anna again. I had a strong hunch about the connections among the three of us, not just Dr. Weiss and myself, but Anna as well. While she was under trance, I asked if she saw a time when we had been together before.

"Yes," she said, "at the healing temple. Dr. Weiss was the elder healer. He had a white beard, long white hair, and wore a long white robe."

I phoned Dr. Weiss and asked if he had ever been regressed to a previous life. He had. In fact, he had seen several lives. At different times he had been a priest, a physician, and a healer. In this context, a "healer" is a person who combines the functions of physician, priest, and teacher. It is a concept common to several ancient societies in Asia, Africa, and Europe. I asked what he knew of his lifetime as a healer.

"Apparently," he said, "I was the elder healer, in a healing temple. I know that the temple had pillars, and I had a long white beard. My hair was long and white, and I wore a long white robe."

"Did the temple have some sort of symbol?"

"Yes, it had a butterfly over the door. And there was a garden in back of the temple."

"Next to the garden," I said, becoming more and more intrigued, "was there a pool where the healers would bathe and refresh themselves at the end of the day?"

"Yes. There *was.* How did you know?"

"I was there! I worked with you." I said. "It was a long time ago."

When at last we met in New York, Dr. Weiss and I felt like two old and dear friends meeting again after a long separation. Perhaps I should say three old friends and colleagues. Anna, after all, had served at the temple and had described my presence there and Dr. Weiss' as well. I had brought her to the meeting in New York. Afterward, she told me she had had a vision as she watched and listened to us talk. Again she saw Dr. Weiss and me back at the garden of the healing temple. The aged healer, Dr. Weiss, was nearing the end of his life, and I was saying to him that it would be difficult to carry on the work without him. He told me not to fret; that the work would continue at a later time; that a future time would come when we would again be working together.

In November, 1992, Dr. Weiss, Dr. Raymond Moody, and I conducted a three-day workshop entitled "The Healing Power of Past-Life Memories." It took place at Edgar Cayce's Association for Research and Enlightenment (A.R.E.) in Virginia Beach, Virginia. Registrants came from Canada, Mexico, and all over the United States. The organizers of the conference wrote to me afterward to say that it was by far one of the most successful programs in the sixty-one-year history of the Association. I subsequently counseled hundreds of patients using past-life therapy.

Dr. Oliver Wendell Holmes observed that "Man's mind, once stretched by a new idea, never regains its original dimensions." At times when all this seems too bizarre to be valid, I remind myself that so did the Copernican concept when people first heard or read of it. The "modern" science of that age "knew" the sun rotated around the earth and the earth was the center of the universe until a new idea stretched the minds of astronomers.

Although Dr. Weiss has broken new ground in this field, so have others, and he is by no means the only physician who has written about healing patients by means of past-life therapy. Other books come to mind: *Coming Back,* by Raymond Moody, M.D., Ph.D.; *Life Between Life,* by Joel Whitten, M.D., Ph.D.; and *Mind Probe Hypnosis,* by Irene Hickman, D.O. I still assessed what portions of my patients' stories might be true past-life memories, personal allegories, imaginations or tap pings into the cosmic consciousness. Meanwhile, my patients improved, at times with incredible speed, and that was what my job was all about.

Sometimes people ask me if this work caused a conflict of conscience with my Catholicism. I had no problem with that (though my pastor might). I see religion as a means to an end. Its goal is the attainment of a connection with God to make this life meaningful and ultimately achieve a higher level of oneness with Him. The Church once persecuted and tortured its members who believed in reincarnation or that the earth was not the center of the universe. In 1992, it officially changed its tenets on the rotation of the planets. Perhaps a hundred years from now it will re-entertain its view of reincarnation. Meanwhile, I feel obligated to make the most of this brain that God gave to me, and not allow my religion to interfere with my spirituality.

Chapter 11

My Own Past Life Visions

In Chapter 9 I told the story of Anna and her past-life experiences. Though I did not know it at the time, when Anna came into my office she opened the door to my understanding of the real purpose of my work. In Chapter 10, I referred briefly to a previous incarnation of my own, which would not have been discovered without Anna's revelations. Let me tell you a bit more about my own past-life experiences and how fate engineered a career focus.

Even before Anna re-experienced her previous lives, there were indications that events prior to her twentieth-century existence were exerting an influence on her. While she was experiencing the cessation of menses and developing the abdominal pain characteristic of ectopic pregnancy, she was also having unexplained emotional reactions. As she came out of deep trance, she would often say, "I'm sorry." When I asked her what she felt sorry about, she did not know. Then, one day after a particularly deep trance, she looked long and pitifully into my eyes and said in a profoundly remorseful tone, "I'm so sorry for what I did to you!"

When I asked her what she meant, she had no idea. I put her back into trance and asked her to *see* why she felt so sorry. This is what she described.

"I see the hands of an old woman. They're raw and shriveled. She's holding a baby ...I love that baby so, I can't stand to hear it cry like this." Anna began to weep as she spoke. "I smell olive oil," she said.

Her reference to olive oil was intriguing. After recent hypnotic sessions, she had told me she detected this odor but did not know where it came from. Scent is something we cannot consciously imagine clearly. For example, you can close your eyes and easily imagine remember and see what a banana looks like, but you cannot clearly imagine its smell. Acute odor awareness is a good indicator that the hypnotic subject is operating at a subconscious level. Now, for the first time, Anna was connecting this odor to a particular scene or event.

"The baby is crying because I have no milk to give it. I'm too old, and it's so tiny."

I felt a deep pity for the pangs of this old woman, and then realized I was becoming emotionally involved in what seemed to be an imaginary scenario. But my patient's sorrow was real. I asked her to describe the setting. It sounded like the Middle East during biblical times. I asked her to see the time and place more precisely, but she was aware only that she was in a village. I asked what her name was, and as I did so, I thought to myself that she would probably come up with the name Sarah to fit the Biblical scene.

"Sarah," she said, and I thought, "I knew it. Now she'll say the baby's name is David." I hesitated to ask her because when she says "David" I'd know I shouldn't have known that. I knew that if I stepped onto that path there would be no going back.

It also occurred to me that perhaps I was getting carried away, experiencing the transference and countertransference of therapist involvement with a patient. But I realized this was only my ploy to avoid or deny what was happening. I knew I had to ask her the child's name, and I knew what her answer would be.

I asked, and she said, "David." My heart sank. She went on to relate the following story.

Because of her age, Sarah was unable to nurse her baby. With her tiny infant crying for nourishment in her arms and the woman heartsick because she could not feed it, she let other women in the village talk her into giving up the child. The baby, they convinced her, would surely die unless Sarah turned it over to them. They could find women to wet-nurse the child if she would allow them to keep it as their own. Sarah hated the prospect of giving up her newborn child and she did not trust these women to care for her son, but she felt she had no choice.

I asked her what became of the child, and she said he was taken to another village where he grew up and eventually worked as a healer. My reaction to her account vacillated between relief, wonder, disbelief, and a sense of foolishness for being so gullible. But what was uppermost in my thoughts was the growing conviction that I was getting into something unexpected and strange, with the potential for discoveries which I felt needed exploration.

When Anna came out of trance and I started to retell her story, she glanced down and felt her blouse. There was a discharge coming from her nipples. She was as dumbfounded as I was. She phoned me later that day to tell me that by the time she had reached home her blouse was soaked.

"What is going on?" she said.

I had no good explanation. She was a nurse and I reminded her of the condition known as pseudocyesis or false pregnancy. Perhaps a very vivid imagination was causing this discharge. There never was any good explanation for this in my medical training, except that it was another example of how the mind and body can operate together. Women, it seemed, were more susceptible than men to manifestations of the close mind/body connection. The ancients believed that a woman's emotions resided in the uterus and the word *hysteria* is derived from the Greek *ysters,* meaning uterus. (The removal of the uterus is called a hysterectomy.) It is interesting that in recent years modern medicine has begun to acknowledge that a woman's emotional state seems to undergo a change after a hysterectomy.

Anna herself was somewhat bewildered but not particularly fearful of whatever was going on. For my part, however, I was wishing that I felt on firmer ground.

As I worked with her over the course of the next few months, more of her past lives surfaced. Her therapy was not very intense, and much of the time I wondered if our sessions were more beneficial for my enlightenment than they were for her. On more than one occasion I mentioned this to Anna. I did not want to take advantage of the situation in any way. However, she always replied that she was very comfortable with what we were doing, was benefitting from it, and if I could derive some benefit too, so much the better.

I had been working with her for almost a year before we heard about Dr. Brian Weiss's research and writings on past-life therapy. After we met, he encouraged me to have my own past-life regression done, as he thought it might help me in my work.

Anna had visualized me in a number of her previous lifetimes, and I was intrigued by the prospect of viewing these for myself.

Shortly after Anna, Brian, and I got together in New York, I received a note from her cancelling her next appointment. She said that, having gotten Brian and me together, she felt her purpose for corning into my life was now fulfilled. It was as if unable to nurture and sustain me in a prior life, she had returned to provide for me what she had failed to do before.

I never saw her again.

However, my efforts at achieving past-life visions of myself were frustrating. I had attempted these regressions on three occasions during mass inductions at past-life seminars, including one conducted by Dr. Weiss at a conference of the Association for Research and Enlightenment. I had yet to experience anything. Then, at that same A.R.E. seminar, Raymond Moody asked if I would do him the favor of regressing him. I did, and afterward he asked if I would like him to reciprocate. As it turned out, he was so exhausted after our session that he had difficulty hypnotizing me, and instead he asked a colleague to do it.

I went into trance rather quickly, and apparently began to see some scenes from the past. I say apparently because, like most subjects' first encounters with these experiences, I had doubts flying in and out of my consciousness. Most people ask themselves, "Am I just making this up-imagining it?" Often, there is no way to tell.

Be that as it may, I saw myself in three distinct lifetimes. One was my life as a healer in the ancient temple where Brian and Anna worked with me, an experience described in Chapter Ten. I saw myself fall over in the garden pool and die of an apparent heart attack sometime after the two others had died. I was weary of the work of healing. I had been working alone and no matter how many of the sick I tended to, there were always more who needed help. I was not sorry to die. It was a relief to know my work was finally over, and I felt joy at seeing those two dear friends waiting for me in the light.

In the scene that came to me from the second life, I was a Union Army surgeon during a Civil War battle. It was a typical combat scene, with wounded men lying on the ground moaning, screaming, and dying. Again I was frustrated and exhausted by my work. I looked across the battlefield and saw, on a farmland hilltop, my medical counterpart in the Confederate forces tending to the soldiers our Union troops had shot. I thought it such a terrible waste. All these young men ought to be back at their own homes, tending their farms, and courting their young ladies instead of destroying one another's lives in this farmer's fields.

I wondered, what if both armies let the medical officers write the orders of the day and plan the campaign strategies? We might simply say, "About face! All you boys just go on home now. It's time again to take part in life; there's no joy in taking part in death. Grow up healthy, take care of yourselves, and have wonderful lives." I thought my Confederate counterpart would probably concur.

Then, as I looked around at our hilltop strewn with dying men, I saw a young soldier lying on the ground, propping himself up on his left elbow. Unlike so many of the other wounded who were moaning or crying out for help, this man had a peaceful smile on his face. It occurred to me when I saw him that this seemed to be a friend of mine, Howard Schnabolk, in my present lifetime as Bob Jarmon. Howard was a wonderful guy who loved life and always had a ready smile for everyone. He went to war in Vietnam, flying medical rescue ("dust-off") helicopters, and was killed there while evacuating wounded soldiers.

I looked into the eyes of the young Union soldier and could not understand how he could be lying there so content with his horrible wound. As I walked over to him, he waved his hand weakly and smiled again in a way that seemed to say, "It's all right, Doc. Don't bother with me. Go tend to the others, the ones who can use your help. I'll be out of this hell soon, and I'm at peace with that."

I fully understood how he felt. As I slowly turned my exhausted body, mind, and soul to care for the next battle victim, I envied him. He was right. He was getting out of hell, while I had to stay.

The third and last scene I saw was as a young man in a Southern state in the early 1800s. I had been a successful merchant, but now I was on my deathbed. My young wife and three small children were at my bedside. I was dying of throat cancer. I had enjoyed smoking big black cigars without a suspicion of any possible health consequences in that era long before medical science had discovered the connection between smoking and disease. The juices from the tobacco had caused cancerous masses to grow in my throat. My wife and children were crying. I was very weak and had great difficulty breathing.

These sensations were so real at the time that I started to have difficulty breathing and felt my throat swelling. I had sufficient conscious awareness to realize that the therapist hypnotizing me was becoming very uneasy about my condition. I sensed a growing anxiety in her voice, and that held me back from going even deeper into my trance. But still the scene was so real and poignant to me that I cried as I have never cried before or since.

As I felt myself die and sensed my soul being released from my body, I was filled with anger at myself for having given myself this disease. I was, after all, seeing the scene from the perspective of my present life, fully aware that tobacco had brought on this cancer. I was not feeling sorry for myself, as I felt that I deserved what was happening. My anger and tears were over what I had done to my beautiful, happy family. Leaving my body, looking down at my innocent, crying children and wife, I vowed with all my soul that I would do whatever I could to prevent this type of tragedy from happening to any other family.

All my life I have disliked the very notion of smoking. It never made sense to me that people would do it. As a child, I used to hide my parents' cigarettes from them. Whenever I saw people smoking, I wanted to approach them and try to talk them out of it. I usually (but not always) managed to control that lifelong urge. The original reason I took up the study of hypnosis in 1978 was to help people break away from nicotine addiction. At the time, I thought my motivation was simply that I had seen too much of its carnage in the form of lung cancer, heart attacks, and emphysema while working in emergency medicine. Through the years, I had developed a reputation as a crusading antismoking doctor. When Ciba-Geigy Pharmaceuticals was planning to market its Habitrol nicotine patch, the company asked me to be one of the physician lecturers who would help to train other physicians to get patients off cigarettes.

Now, my intense, negative feelings about watching people smoke made sense to me in a new and stronger way. My analytical and skeptical mind, however, questioned whether my imagination had merely concocted this tale of a cigar-smoking father of three to explain to myself why I am so fervent in my attacks on smoking.

To which I must honestly answer: perhaps.

But during my hypnotic regression, my throat certainly felt as if it were closing over, and I was enraged to tears over what I had done to my family. Whether it was imagination or a view of the painful ending of a past life, I saw the long-term effects of nicotine so vividly that I never feel qualms about pressuring smokers to quit.

Two years later, I was back at the A.R.E. in Virginia Beach, this time as a lecturer at a reincarnation program which I helped to initiate. Brian Weiss also participated in the program. As he usually does on such occasions, he led the audience into a group regression. At one point he instructed us to see where we were in the year 1870.

Immediately I saw myself as that weary physician who had survived the Civil War. He told us to seek a sense of how that previous existence might relate to our current lives. Instantly I was struck by a concept which has profound meaning for me. That nineteenth-century surgeon and that ancient healer had both led laborious, very frustrating, if occasionally gratifying lives. Physicians who only take care of the physical body are inevitably frustrated. All of our best work is ultimately futile. At best, medicine fights a delaying action. Death sooner or later finds us all. However, if your work is focused on the soul, the progress may be permanent.

Chapter 12

A Reunion of Comrades in Arms

Sometimes therapy can reach beyond the person in the consultation room

As a rule, time in my consultation room is devoted strictly to patients in need of therapy, but there have been exceptions. On one such occasion, a man I will call Joe made an appointment for no more urgent a reason than to discuss my views about reincarnation, or so he and I both thought. As it turned out, because of our meeting he was able to help an old man peacefully deal with the prospect of death, or more accurately, that it was his long-dead grandfather who helped.

At the time of our meeting, Joe was forty years old, a successful litigation attorney, husky, well-spoken, happily married, the father of two children. Some twenty years earlier, while studying comparative religion in college, he had become interested in the concept of reincarnation. On an intuitive level, it seemed to him to ring true, but his interest had been mild, more or less sporadic, and he had never explored the possibility of his own past lives.

Then, quite recently, a friend had given him a copy of *Many Lives, Many Masters* the book in which Dr. Brian Weiss writes of his psychotherapeutic encounters with a patient's past lives. Fascinated by the accounts, he contacted the author's office in Miami and asked to be referred to a like-minded psychiatrist in New Jersey. He was given my name and location, and called me. Dr. Weiss and I had discovered that we shared some fascinating pasts (see Chapter Ten). Joe told me how long he had been interested in the subject and added that although he had no problems requiring counseling, he felt strongly that he was meant to pursue his old interest again at this time.

Generally I do not work with those who are simply curious about past lives. But occasionally I sense that something there needs to be given attention. This time my sense was, "See this one."

Accompanied by his wife, Joe arrived a few minutes early, and read some of my office literature while waiting to see me. I brought him into my consultation room and reviewed his life history and current situation. Nothing in Joe's life indicated the need for therapy. There was only one unhappy situation bothering him, and it was not his own. An eighty-year-old gentleman named Sal, who had been working for him for many years, was rapidly showing the signs of age that precede the end of a long life. Sal felt that he had at most a few years left, and had become extremely despondent at the prospect of impending death.

Sal and Joe's grandfather, Vincent, had emigrated from Italy together as young boys, had grown up together in New Jersey, had weathered the Great Depression together, and had served in the army together. They had been the closest of friends, and Vincent's death in the 1960s was a very hard blow for Sal. Before he died, Vincent had asked Sal to look after his grandson Joey, and had asked Joe in turn to look after Sal. Joe had always done that to the best of his ability, but now he could find no way to give Sal hope or consolation in facing old age and the end of his life.

Sal's health was failing steadily, and he was becoming clinically depressed. Unfortunately, he was the kind of person who scoffed at psychotherapy and would never consider seeing a counselor. Unlike Vincent, he had chosen to remain in the army when World War II ended and had made a career of soldiering. As a retired army man, he regarded himself as tough and cynical, too worldly and wise to be taken in by "shrinks." He had no more use for religion than for psychiatry. Never having shared his friend Vincent's spiritual convictions, and with his life coming to a close, he felt the hopelessness and isolation of the atheist who has "no invisible means of support." Thus, Joe could find no way or words to comfort his beloved grandfather's old friend.

After discussing this and other matters with me for some time, Joe mentioned that he had practiced self-hypnosis and meditation, and he suggested that I hypnotize him in order to see if regression might lead to any significant discoveries. We went back through his childhood, and along the way he recalled in more detail conversations with the grandfather about watching over Sal who was not, in Vincent's estimation, quite as self-sufficient as he wished to appear.

Stage by stage, Joe's memories under hypnosis took him back through puberty, into early childhood, into infancy, and then before entry into his present life, to a resting place of peaceful floating and light. Abruptly, he regressed still farther, his mind leaping from that resting place to another life, the life of a soldier of ancient Rome. A good friend from his present lifetime was with him there too, as a comrade in arms. Together they fought and died for Rome while relatively young.

When Joe stopped speaking, I brought him forward again in time, but as I did so he interrupted to describe a new vision. His grandfather appeared and told Joe that Joey was also a warrior but of a different kind, without resort to force or violence; that he would do better now to become a healer of some sort, a solver of people's problems. It occurred to me that this description could fit his current role as an attorney. I thought of a friend of mine who quit law practice because he had disliked being just a "hired gun".

Then something else occurred to me. I asked if his grandfather did not also have some message for his old friend Sal, something that might comfort the man at this unhappy period of his waning life. Still in trance, Joe sat silent for a few seconds and then began to describe another vision, a scene from his grandfather's youth.

Vincent and Sal were young men, walking in a park late at night. Sal was telling his friend about a family vendetta that he had thought was left behind in Italy, until he discovered that immigrants had brought the hatred with them across the ocean. Sal's life had been threatened, and the threat was the type to be taken seriously.

Vincent was normally not a violent man, but he WAS a man of unshakable loyalty. He would take care of the situation. "No", Sal told him, he must not; this was something he would have to do for himself. He was grateful to his friend, but adamant, and he swore Vincent to secrecy.

"What happened?" I asked. "Did Sal carry on the vendetta? Was anyone hurt?" But Joe knew nothing more about it. There were no further visions or recollections.

When I brought him out of his deep trance, he remembered everything he had told me. I asked if Vincent or Sal had ever mentioned that incident. "No", he had never known anything about it and had never even been aware that Sal had any enemies.

"Joe," I said, "if it really happened the way you visualized it, and no one but your grandfather and Sal ever knew about it, this might be just what Sal needs to hear. A demonstration to him that something does exist beyond the grave could be a source of comfort." Joe agreed that it could be a sort of spiritual tonic for Sal, but perhaps it was all just a product of wishful thinking. He thanked me and said he would keep in touch. Three days later he phoned.

"Just wanted you to know how good I've been feeling. I really needed to deal with this reincarnation concept. I seem to have a different perspective now, but I have something more important I want to tell you about. I had a talk with Sal. I didn't tell him I went to a psychiatrist. That would have just put him off. I told him I'd had a really strange dream and then I described the vision I had in your office, about Grandpa and Sal walking in the park. You should have seen his face when I came to the part about the vendetta. He said to me, 'How could you dream that? We never told anybody.'"

Joe said, "Well, it must have been in my subconscious."

"It couldn't have come from your subconscious, because you never knew about it, so it was never there in the first place."

"I guess I was just as surprised as Sal was. So I asked him, 'Then it's true?'"

"'Yeah, it's true. I just don't understand it.' Sal didn't seem to want to talk about it anymore. He went for a walk and didn't come back for quite a while. Then he just sat around all evening, looking into space. Maybe he was just thinking about old times, but I don't think so. I think it did him good. I'll watch him and let you know how he acts."

I heard nothing more for a couple of months, and then Joe called me again to let me know everything was fine. Sal's health was still deteriorating, but his troubled expression had been gone ever since their conversation about Joe's grandfather. Sal had attained a peace with himself and the world.

Chapter 13

A Lonely Shepherd's Promise

An Old Promise Kept

We all know that appearances can be deceiving, but sometimes what lies beneath a patient's physical appearance and demeanor can be totally unexpected. Eileen was thirty years old, the mother of three children; a very plain-looking, overweight woman whose only physically attractive aspect, or so it would seem, was her red hair. She did not conform to our society's view of feminine physical beauty, nor was her personality or intellect of the sort that would captivate a handsome, well-educated, energetic, and ambitious young man. Nonetheless, she said just such a man was a central part of her problem, and that his obsession with her would be problematic for him as well.

She came to my office to seek relief from chronic depression which seemed at first to stem from her lot in life. She had grown up in a blue-collar Irish neighborhood in a large industrial city. Her husband, family, and friends were blue-collar workers with little formal education and few interests outside of their community: sports, playing the lottery, and enjoying an occasional night out. Like her family and friends, she had no aspirations beyond the life she knew and might have been moderately content with her home situation but for one tormenting secret passion.

For seven years, she had been having an illicit affair with a thirty-year old college-educated Jewish stockbroker. She and her lover, Stephen, both knew that their families would disown them if their affair was revealed, and neither of them could have accepted those consequences.

Eileen was profoundly and painfully aware of how ill-suited they were for each other. They did not share a single common interest. They did not view life, success, or happiness in the same way. They did not fully understand each other's deepest concerns. Even their manner of speaking was totally different. She described him to me, not with pride or happiness, but with bewilderment.

She said he was tall, very handsome, well dressed and professional looking, extremely successful in his brokerage business. He had never married, and she said he had told her he could not because of his infatuation with her. Far from pleasing her, this situation seemed to make her all the more miserable. She felt that the only way they both could be happy would be if he would just let go of her and get on with his life. Then she could let go of him and get on with hers. It was as if they were chained to each other. Her plight, their plight, seemed hopeless to her.

I listened attentively trying to communicate understanding and sympathy, but I was skeptical of her story. The more details she added to her description of him and her account of their mutual infatuation, the more it sounded to me like the confabulation of a bored, frustrated young house-wife's wishful thinking. I thought this was likely a the daydream fantasy that might be spawned by television soap operas or paperback romances. If Stephen were really so wonderful, why would he be so obsessed with this rather unappealing woman?

That was my first reaction. My second was to chide myself for being judgmental. After all, in matters of taste there is no right or wrong. Plus, I should keep an open mind while helping the patient sort out her situation.

I did what I could in terms of counseling, and hoped for more developments from her next visit. We had two more sessions but seemed to be making little or no progress in relieving her deep depression. At one point, she described Stephen to me as her "soul mate", but that strange soul mate's love gave her no contentment. It only made her unhappy and fearful of losing what happiness she had with her family. In spite of the misery and fear, she could not and would not let him go, and I was compelled to point that out. This, she said, she knew very well. It was why she had sought my help. She *wanted* to let him go and was desperately looking for some way out.

During her third session with me, she asked if I thought it

might be helpful for me to see Stephen in therapy. Good idea. Here, I felt, was a young man who needed help as much as she did. Besides, I wanted to meet him and see if he was really was as she had described.

I was not sure he would call for an appointment. I was not even sure he existed. He called that very evening. When he arrived for his appointment, I was surprised to see that he was all she had said he was: tall, handsome, well-built with dark, curly hair, impeccably dressed, well-spoken, polite, and self-assured. He exuded confidence and control. He did not seem to be the kind of man who would desire to be with a woman who displayed so little charm. I was even more puzzled.

His story accorded exactly with hers. He felt bound to Eileen, could not fathom why, and wished to be free. Except for his inexplicable fixation on this plain-looking, rather dull, and uncultured mother of three, he seemed more well-adjusted than most people. In fact, he struck me as a rather intuitive, ambitious, aggressive young man on his way up in the world. Inquiring about his involvement with her, I asked as tactfully as I could, what he saw in this woman.

Indeed, he told me he had been struggling with that quandary for seven years. Far from idealizing her, he was blunt, almost resentful in talking about Eileen. "I know," he said, "she's not very bright, and she acts a little neurotic. She's not even good looking. I could do a lot better. I mean, I'm not bragging, I've had plenty of other opportunities. But I just feel as if I have to be around her, almost as if I have to take care of her, that I have some kind of duty, some obligation. She and I have talked about that. It sounds ridiculous, I guess, but we've told each other it feels like a left over connection from some other lifetime. We've talked about it again and again. Makes no sense, does it?"

We had four more sessions during which we examined every aspect of the relationship and any detectable, motivating factors, conscious or unconscious. The puzzle remained. I had only recently begun to explore and make use of past-life therapy and still was not sure what to make of it, but if ever there was a case that seemed appropriate for this therapeutic modality, surely this was one. I decided to suggest it.

"I've had some patients," I said, "who found a resolution to problems or symptoms when I put them into hypnotic trance and they visualized scenes that appeared to be from another lifetime. I'm not prepared to tell you whether the images they see are real events from previous lives or just figments of their imaginations. It doesn't really matter as long as the experience provides insights into problems and helps resolve issues. What I'm getting at is that I suspect we might find hypnotic regression useful for you. How do you feel about it?"

"Why not?", he said. "I'll try anything that might end this thing. I've really got to get free. Hell, so does Eileen."

Although he had never previously been hypnotized, he accepted the procedure easily and soon went into deep trance. I then directed him to travel back in time and place to where he was previously connected to Eileen or Eileen's soul, to the situation which carried over into his current life.

Within just a few moments, his facial expression began to change. It went from peaceful to anguished, and then, quite abruptly, he began to weep. There in my office this man, whose composure had seemed so unbreakable, was suddenly and uncontrollably sobbing. As he cried, he was talking to an imagined young woman, an invisible girl he was cradling in his arms. I could tell that much, but I could not understand his words; he was speaking a foreign language.

I was able, gently, to break in on the scene he was visualizing, and I began to question him. He replied in English, and his story began to unfold. He was, he told me, an eighteen-year old shepherd living near the Mediterranean coast. He was in love with a young woman of his village, and they had planned their marriage with the blessing of both families. But she had become ill and began to waste away. It sounded to me as if she was suffering from cancer. Then, she was dying in his arms as he begged her not to leave him. She was apologizing to him! She was telling him how sorry she was for the pain her death would bring him. He cried as all of this came back to him. With heart-wrenching sobs, he promised to be with her again.

Just as I had been initially skeptical when Eileen told me about Stephen, now I felt myself wondering whether I was hearing fact or neurotic fantasy. On the other hand, if he was processing a grief reaction and having a healing catharsis (a delayed emotional expression), it could be counterproductive for me to squash it by expressing skepticism.

I guided him forward in time through that incarnation. He told me that he had lived into old age and lived a dull and sorrowful lifetime, never marrying, mourning for the woman he would have married. It was time to bring him forward into his present life, hopefully free of his emotional bondage.

While still under hypnosis I told him, "Her body from that past life is dead. You could never have prevented her death and you honored your commitment to her longer than was needed. Her soul long ago went on to the resting place and has come back now in another body. But she's a different person, her life is different now, and it can be a contented life. It wasn't your fault that she died. Eventually, you died, too, and came back. You kept your promise, you met her again and that frees you both. You're free of those obligations formed in an earlier lifetime. It's time for you to go your separate ways. She has her mate, she'll have contentment without you, and you need to find your new mate in the present, in your current life."

As I heard myself saying those words, I also imagined a small voice inside my head ridiculing me, telling me I sounded like some mystical guru and asking where in my medical training I had absorbed such concepts. In those years, I was still very uneasy with this strange therapeutic approach.

I brought Stephen out of trance and asked him how he felt. For a few moments, he was slightly groggy, but soon became alert and intensely interested in what had just transpired. I asked him if he was aware of what he had said.

"Yes," he said. "Well, vaguely."

I told him in detail what he had described. "What now?" he asked. "What does it mean? I can see what it says about Eileen and me, but is it real? I don't know if I can accept it. What do you think, Doctor, will we be free now?"

"I can't answer you for certain," I admitted. "If it resolves your dilemma, you're cured. If not, we have more work to do." (Well, I thought, at least that sounds more like a standard psychotherapeutic response – be as non-committal as the English language allows)

Before leaving the office, he made an appointment to see me again the following Thursday, as usual. But two days later, he phoned to cancel the appointment. He was about to leave town briefly. He had run into an old girlfriend; they had immediately felt a strong mutual attraction, and they were off for a week of skiing in New England. He said, "She was bright, beautiful, and fascinating -- the antithesis of Eileen." Perhaps his comparison was callous, but if so, it indicated that the shackles had been broken.

"What about Eileen?" I asked.

"She's fine," he said. "Doesn't even want to see me. I'm not sure what happened in your office, and maybe I'll never know. But it's very strange, I don't feel any attachment to her at all. Nothing, ancient history. So whatever you did, thanks. Eileen thanks you, too. I'll certainly know to call you if I ever need help again."

That was many years ago. I have not heard from either of them since.

Chapter 14

A Mother's Abandonment Karma

In this book, I have written about the soul and past-life therapy, and presented a number of case studies which, I hope, have been illuminating with regard to these concepts. I have also written briefly of karma, the principle of causality in Hinduism and Buddhism. As stated elsewhere in this book, karma has been defined as the resultant ethical consequences of one's acts that fix ones lot in the future existence; the continuous working of every thought, word, or deed throughout eternity in a causal sequence. Karmic commentaries and interpretations have filled books, and the definition just offered is necessarily only a basic and simple one, but it has direct application to the healing of the soul.

It is unfortunate that so many people define it in an even simpler way, as one's unchangeable destiny, as if a person cannot and should not take responsibility for his or her actions and his or her future fate. On the contrary, our thoughts, words, and acts directly influence what is to come in this present life and in future incarnations just as our thoughts, words, and deeds in previous lives influence our present incarnation. Belief in the karmic journey of the soul, with accompanying insight into its ramifications, has been a balm for some of my patients. These journeys do not lend themselves to scientific proof, but the concept lends itself to the healing of anguish.

One patient brought an insight that cannot be proven but could bring peace and healing to families mourning the deaths of infants.

This patient was Cathy, forty-two years old, the mother of four, and newly divorced. She had come to me for help in resigning herself to her broken marriage so that she could get on with her life. She was only slightly co-dependent in her relationship with her former husband, Fred, but she was a caregiver by nature and had difficulty turning away from anyone who needed help.

Clearly discernible beneath Fred's affable surface was a very troubled soul. He suffered from alcoholism and manic/depressive or bipolar disorder. Cathy had stayed with him as long as she could bear to. Al-anon guidelines would have labeled her efforts to help him as "enabling;" that is, enabling him to continue his drinking and excusing or denying his condition rather than letting him deal alone with the consequences of his actions. "Tough love," loving a person enough to be tough with him and tolerate no further misconduct, does not come easily. Family life and finances had deteriorated until there had been no rational alternative to divorce, and very soon after Fred was gone, Cathy came into therapy.

After a session of cognitive-logic-oriented-counseling, Cathy knew clearly what mental steps she had to take to proceed with her life, but her emotional attachment to Fred was not so easily broken. She felt rather as if she had abandoned him. I suggested hypnosis to help her visualize getting on in life without him.

She had had experience with meditation and was able to get into clinical hypnosis quickly. I directed her to go back to the reason why she felt so forcefully compelled to take care of Fred. Her facial expression became intense, and for about half a minute, she wept. When her sobbing stopped, her expression changed abruptly, first to a look of surprise and then relief and peace.

"Oh, my God!" she exclaimed, "It's Fred. My baby is Fred!"

"Your baby?", I said. "What do you see? What do you see happening?" As she explained what she saw, I found the scenario at first surprising but revealing, and then bewildering.

In another lifetime, she had been an expectant mother, and when she returned to that previous lifetime she saw herself dying in childbirth. She also sensed that the infant survived. It was a boy. She immediately realized that it was Fred in a previous incarnation. Quite frequently, people who visualize themselves in past lives also visualize past-life connections with previous incarnations of present-life relatives, loved ones, or friends. That much I understood, and was only momentarily surprised. But then she uttered an astonishing and perplexing statement

"I wanted to stay. How I wanted to stay, to watch over him. But I had to go. He wasn't even two years old when I had to leave."

I was somewhat confused. How, I wondered, if she had died in childbirth, had she stayed to watch over her son until he was almost two years old? I asked her what she meant by "staying" and "watching over" the infant. She explained almost matter-of-factly that her soul had resisted going to the light, had struggled to remain on the earth plane in order to be with him and guard him. She had felt deeply guilty for dying as he was born and, thus, "deserting" him. But in time, the spirit guides had persuaded or somehow commanded her to depart and go to the resting place.

This, it seemed, would be a useful perspective for her to understand why she had needed to go on caring for her husband, the reincarnation of the son she had borne. I offered healing affirmations that she could not have prevented her own death. It was not her fault she had left her baby, and that she had sought him out again in this present life in order to give him help that she had not been able to provide in that previous lifetime. She had now given all the help that could be given, except for one last act which was to let him go. Let him go out into the world without further mothering, on his own, to learn the lessons that only his own experiences could provide.

Whether or not all this was absolutely true in a factual sense, she clearly seemed to be accepting it and was enormously relieved. She was healing, and that was what she had come for. But something occurred to me and I decided not to bring her out of trance quite yet. What if I had before me a mind, conscious, or subconscious, that possessed some knowledge of death and the afterlife, the soul's experience of survival and subsequent lives and deaths. Perhaps she could answer some questions for me about S.I.D.S. I'll describe that conversation in another chapter.

Out of Body Experiences - OBEs

Chapter 15

Does No One out there Love Me?

Having a Reason to Live

The OBEs are somewhat similar to the near-death experiences described in the previous chapters, but there are significant differences. The experience may occur with or without the prospect of imminent death, and there is no passing into the tunnel of light, no perceived figures or beings directing the spirit back to the body as in accounts of NDE. Instead, the subjects simply perceive themselves leaving their bodies and going elsewhere. The out-of-body self may journey only a few feet, hovering briefly behind or above the body, or may travel hundreds or thousands of miles before returning to a normal state. The first question is whether the phenomenon is real or imagined. It is easy enough to imagine yourself in a place other than where you are. For example, just close your eyes and picture yourself lying relaxed on a warm beach. Interestingly, there are a few people who have difficulty doing that, but most of us can easily imagine ourselves being elsewhere. What can distinguish OBEs from mere imaginings is the intensity with which the person believes positively or knows he or she has left the body.

But this brings up a second, related question: Was the vividly remembered OBE real or could it have been a psychotic state of detachment? A profound sense of detachment can be a symptom of severe mental disturbance. Perhaps the mind just fills in the blanks the way it does in speed reading. A patient is likely to be understandably reluctant to reveal an out-of-body experience for fear that it will be regarded as a hallucinatory sign of psychotic detachment. For the same reasons, therapists should be wary of these accounts. I believe that in some cases OBEs do occur.

If you accept the reality of NDEs, there is no reason not to believe in OBEs. In both phenomena, the spirit, or some of it temporarily leaves the body; even if the circumstances are different. Moreover, clinical findings support the logic of belief.

There have been cases in which the person brought back some information that he or she could not otherwise have known. There have also been cases in which physical or physiological changes immediately followed an OBE.

OBEs may occur with or without apparent cause. Some people report that they wake up in the middle of the night to find themselves floating above their bodies. Some have said that with concentration and practice, they have learned to will themselves into this state. They often describe the experience as fascinating but frightening. A major fear is that perhaps they will not be able to get back into their bodies. Another is that, while the spirit is out of the body, another spirit might enter and occupy it.

One of my patients had an emotional and physical healing as a result of his OBE. Mike was a young truck driver brought to the emergency department of my hospital years ago when I was working in emergency medicine.

Mike was in the intensive care unit and in very unstable condition. Four days earlier, he had been driving his car while drunk, crashed into a tree, and nearly died. The surgeons had inserted a tube into the right side of his chest to re-expand his collapsed lung. He had an intravenous infusion line in his left arm and another intravenous line through which a catheter fed into his heart to measure the delicate pressures within his heart chambers. There was a nasogastric tube attached to a suction bottle and leading through his nose into his stomach to decompress any distention and monitor for bleeding. In addition, a urinary bladder catheter was in place to help measure kidney function and monitor for possible urinary tract bleeding. He did not think he was going to leave the hospital alive.

Upon his initial evaluation and stabilization in the emergency department, he had been told he was about to be taken to the operating room for exploratory abdominal surgery. He had insisted on phoning his wife before signing the consent form and the staff had overheard him talking to her.

"Honey, I'm sorry. I'm sorry for all the grief I've been causing you and the kids. I've messed up our lives, and now it's too late. I'm not gonna make it out of here. I just want you to know I'm sorry."

Four days later, he still doubted that he would make it home, and so did his doctors. He was not fighting to survive. He reminded me of research I had once done regarding the brain-washing of American prisoners of war during the Korean conflict. The goals of that brainwashing included the removal of the will of the captured soldiers to survive. A physically healthy prisoner might go off and sit in a comer, become more and more listless until finally he curled up in a fetal position and within hours die from no apparent physical cause. Mike seemed to have given up in the same manner, and no intravenous tubes or surgical procedures could restore his will to live.

At the age of thirty-four, he saw no reason to continue his existence, and it seemed as if his accident had given him an excuse to quit life. His problems had started very early. He had been the oldest of six children whose alcoholic father had deserted the family when he was eleven years old. His mother could not care for and support six children. The aunt and uncle to whom he was sent let him know very clearly that they had all the responsibility they wanted with their own children and strongly resented his presence. Their home was squalid and unloving, and at the age of twelve he had run away to begin a life on the streets. By the time he was grown and married, he was an alcoholic. The night of his accident had not been the first time he had driven drunk, but it seemed it would be the last.

Human beings seem to have two very strong emotional drives: the need to be loved and the need to be needed. During his childhood and adolescence, Mike had experienced no fulfillment of either. Now he had a wife and three children who loved and needed him but like many people who have been emotionally impoverished or abused in youth, he had not fully accepted their love. Maybe he felt he could not trust it or be worthy of it. He had distanced himself from his wife and children and retreated into the haze of alcohol. He had even abused them, both verbally and physically. Having known no kindness as a child, he had great difficulty expressing kindness to others. So, as he lay near death, he must have been thinking that his life had been little more than a painful waste.

Four days after surgery, the doctors felt he should be showing significant improvement. Medically, there was no reason not to expect him to recover. Yet, his pulse was weak and rapid, his blood pressure dangerously low, his skin ashen, and his lungs still labored to pump badly needed oxygen into his blood. On the sole basis of trauma, the doctors could not explain his failure to show improvement by that morning, nor would they be able to explain his very sudden improvement by the end of that same day.

The change was noticed by the nursing staff very soon after a five minute visit by his brother, George. Within twenty minutes after George's visit, Mike's blood pressure climbed back to near-normal, his pulse slowed and strengthened, his breathing eased, and his skin regained color. About all the attending doctors could say was, "Who knows why or how? Sometimes we get lucky, and that's just the way it happens."

If I had never seen Mike again, I could not have explained his miraculously swift turn for the better and his subsequent recovery. But I did see him, years later, and perhaps because I was now doing counseling, he decided to confide what had happened that day. He had always viewed himself as worthless and unworthy of love. He had been conscious when his brother George came to his bedside that day. Suddenly he felt himself to be about six feet outside of his body, watching and listening to himself and his brother.

George had clutched at Mike's chest as he pleaded with him in an impassioned voice, "Mike, for God's sake, don't die! You can't die. Sheila and the kids need you. Damn it, Mike, your family needs you. They love you, Mike, and you're not gonna let them down, you hear me?"

Mike told me he had never in his life experienced anything like the emotion he felt as he listened and looked down at his brother and himself. He had never thought his life had any value at all, yet, he knew instantly that what his brother was saying was true. His family loved and needed him. He realized as never before, that his life had a purpose and now he *wanted* to live.

"It was strange," he told me, "really weird. I never experienced anything like that before, and you're the first person I've ever told. I've never even told my wife. I mean, I was actually outside of my body, looking down at it, looking down at my brother, listening to both of us. George was crying. I never saw him cry before. If he'd ever said anything like that before, I wouldn't have listened. I never talked about this because I figured people would think I was crazy, or maybe drunk again. But after George's visit, I knew I had some kind of future."

There is a little more to Mike's story, and I think it worth telling. After recuperating from the accident, he joined Alcoholics Anonymous and has stayed sober. He became a sponsor for other alcoholics. No longer abusive, he has developed into a caring husband and father. He still makes occasional mistakes, as do we all, but not as frequently or seriously as he did before his strange experience. He and his brother George have started their own business and are working hard together to make it a success.

Years have passed since Mike's accident, and he has yet to have another out-of-body experience. Perhaps he never will. That single episode of literally stepping aside and taking a good look at himself, was what he needed to begin building his life at the age of thirty-four. At last he had acknowledged and accepted love, and realized his existence was not purposeless. For Mike, love and purpose were truly a matter of life and death.

Chapter 16

PLEASE Tell Mother

A friend of mine told me how one morning he felt an uneasy sensation that his mother needed help. He imagined he saw her lying on a sofa in her living-room, sick or injured. When he drove over to her residence, he discovered that she had suffered a heart attack and had been rushed to a hospital. She had, indeed, been stricken as she entered her living room from her bedroom, and had managed to phone for an ambulance before collapsing onto the sofa. A paramedic team had saved her life. No one had called him, he just "knew".

One morning in 1979 my brother suddenly woke up at 6:30 A.M. with a terrible pain in his chest and trouble breathing. In another part of the state I woke up at the same time with the same symptoms. Our father was in the hospital recovering from pneumonia and a mild heart attack, but was expected to be discharged that day. It was at that moment that he unexpectedly died.

Such incidents are not uncommon, but how is this information transmitted? Incidents of this kind are often ascribed to telepathy, a mental transference of information or emotion from one person to another across space and through barriers, without speech or any mechanical means of communication. Perhaps some portion of a person's spirit energy temporarily leaves the body and travels to the person who receives the message.

I find the following account all the more intriguing because the man who wrote it does not accept the existence of the soul. When he offered to let me use the account of his experience in this book, he commented that he is, at most, an agnostic still looking for answers and not ready to adhere to any particular system of belief. He has no explanation for what happened to him and simply leaves its interpretation to the reader. Here is his account.

"I had been suffering from what proved to be an incipient case of kidney stones for almost two years when I experienced a severe attack. My wife and I were employed as teachers in an American high school at a U.S. military base overseas, and were back in the States for the summer. Soon after we had arrived at my parents' home in New Jersey, the malady struck.

My father lay near death from cancer, my mother was greatly distraught, and now I was ill. In an effort to spare my bride of less than two years the stress occasioned by these unfortunate circumstances, I persuaded her to pay an early visit to her mother in the South. It was a decision I soon regretted. Several days after she left, my condition grew worse, and I was admitted to the local hospital for testing. My father fell into coma, my pain became excruciating, and I became profoundly depressed. I felt an overwhelming need for my wife.

I suppose I might have had someone telephone her, but after all, I was the one who had persuaded her to leave about a week before. I did not want to seem weak and vacillating. I fancied myself a stoic. It would be better, I thought, if she decided on her own to return.

I was scheduled for surgery in three days. That evening as I lay awake in the dimly lighted room, I remembered how I had called out to my mother as I lay feverishly ill in the sick bay of a naval vessel fourteen years earlier. I remembered how my mother on that same evening dreamed that I called to her and knew that I was ill. Now I made a concentrated effort to reach out to my wife.

I imagined that I left my body and seemed to rise toward the ceiling, looking down at myself still lying in bed. I felt myself leave the hospital room through the closed window and travel through the air, seeing the changing landscape from New Jersey to the South as if from a plane.

I came to my mother-in-law's house, descended into it, and stood at the foot of my wife's bed. I called her name and she opened her eyes.

I said, "Come back to me. I need you."

Two days later, I was astonished and deeply gratified to see my wife walk into my room. I asked her why she had come and if anyone had called her.

She replied, "You called me two nights ago. I awoke and saw

you at the foot of my bed. You told me to come back. You said you needed me."

Only then, when she told me of her experience, did I tell her what I had done.

Years later, I confided to my mother this strange episode of my wife's hospital visit. I told her how I was prompted to reach out to my wife based on that incident in the Navy when Mother dreamt that I had called to her.

My mother stopped and corrected me. She said, "No, I didn't just dream that. I tried to tell you at the time but you weren't about to believe me. I told you that I woke up in the night and saw you standing at the foot of my bed. You said, 'Mom, I'm very sick!' That's how I knew to contact you."

Those words, "Mom, I'm very sick!" were exactly the words I remembered calling out from my bed in the ship's sick bay.

You can, of course, simply call these episodes telepathy (whatever that is) and think no further about the actual experiences as related by those who lived them. But that does not adequately explain how the mother of a young man on a naval vessel saw him at the foot of the bed and heard the very words he called out. It does not explain how, fourteen years later, the same man experienced himself leaving his body and traveling a thousand miles from New Jersey to Louisiana to stand at the bed of his sleeping wife and summon help from a loved one once again; or how his wife saw him there and heard his voice, his exact words. It would seem that this man had not one but two out-of-body experiences, both of which brought loving support when he needed it the most.

Chapter 17

DON'T Tell Mother

Eavesdropper

Occasionally, someone came to me for help with a seemingly simple problem, and unexpectedly revealed a quite different and deeper concern or an experience that would change the patient's life. My case files included dozens of patients who had near-death experiences (NDEs) and out-of-body experiences (OBEs), as they have come to be known. Some patients suppressed these experiences, erased them from conscious memory, so that the phenomenon came to light only in the course of hypnosis for other problems. I have also had patients who consciously remembered it all but never spoke of it for fear of ridicule.

Some patients experienced both NDE and OBE, and certain attitudes on life were changed.

A case in point was a man I shall call Harry, a phone company executive in his early fifties who came to me for support in breaking the smoking habit. During the first few minutes of our first session, it became obvious that he was resisting my counseling, to say nothing of hypnotic induction. Quite often, a smoker asks for help without genuinely wanting it; what such a patient really consciously and/ or subconsciously wants is a quick failure of therapy. Without any feeling of guilt, he can then tell himself, his family, and others that he really did try and "even went to a hypnotist", but his case is hopeless, the addiction too strong.

I suspected that Harry was that kind of self-vindicating smoker, and I suggested to him that perhaps he was not fully cooperative because he was not yet ready to give up cigarettes.

"No, Doc," he said, "it's not that, believe me. I'm ready to quit, all right. I've gotten to the point where I don't even *like* cigarettes, and I know what they're doing to me. So believe me, it's not that. It's not you. I mean, not you personally. It's just, well, it's a little embarrassing to tell you this but I guess I've got to say it, got to clear the air, you know? The fact is, I'm sorry, Doc, but I don't much like doctors. I guess I just don't trust them. Not any of them."

"Did something happen to make you feel that way?" I asked. "Did you have a bad experience?"

"Well, I had an operation once, and it didn't go too well. Look, I know it's stupid to generalize, but I don't think I'll ever feel really confident with a physician again. I guess you could say I'm a little scared of them. Do I want to quit smoking? Well, I came here, didn't I? I *hate* going to doctors. The trouble is, now I'm here, I can't seem to relax and let you help me."

"I think you should tell me what happened," I said. "Tell me about the operation. If that's a block, we need to clear it away so you *can* let me help you."

Hesitantly at first, he related the following story. He had gone into the hospital for a simple hernia repair. His wife had accompanied him, and was sitting in a waiting room. They had both been assured the surgery would be simple and relatively fast, and she could see him after he was brought from the recovery room. She was a little nervous, but not afraid, and he was not worried at all.

"But something went wrong," he told me. "I didn't know what it was, but afterward they told me I'd gone into cardiac arrest. All of a sudden I seemed to be floating. Sounds crazy, doesn't it? I was floating above my own body, watching all the activity. The doctors and nurses were yelling, and the nurses were rushing around. The surgeon was yelling at the anesthesiologist that he'd given me too much anesthesia, and the anesthesiologist was yelling 'The hell I did,' and telling the surgeon he was screwing up the resuscitation.

"I could hear everything, and I was thinking, 'Don't you dumb bastards know what you're doing?' To me, they looked like they were out of control. Here they are, arguing about how come they're losing a patient, and I'm the patient they're losing."

Then he added another interesting bit of information: "I didn't have so much confidence in my wife's judgment after that, either."

"Your wife?". I said. "What did she have to do with it?"

"Well, first, you see, I was floating up there, looking down on myself and the doctors. But then I floated away. I felt like I needed to see my wife, and I floated right out of the operating room, right down the hallway. There was my wife on the pay phone, calling my mother. I couldn't believe it. She's found out it isn't going right and she's in a panic and telling my mother all about it. You think I was having hallucinations, right, Doc?"

"No," I assured him, "I've heard stranger things. I've had other patients tell me about near-death experiences, floating above their own bodies and then coming back. Go on, tell me the rest."

"Well, what happened was they'd told my wife there were complications. They said I was in cardiac arrest and they were trying everything but it didn't look good. So my wife was frantic and she was babbling all about it to my mother while there I was, floating above her. I could hear that my mother was not believing it. She was insisting it was just a simple operation and what could go wrong? I don't know what my wife said after that, because the next thing I knew I was floating up higher, up into some kind of tunnel of light. Then there was some figure in a white robe. I couldn't tell you what his face looked like, it was just this figure in white, telling me I had to go back, that it wasn't my time. Here's something really weird, Doc, I knew it was right, that I had to go back, but I almost regretted it. I mean, going back to life with all the pain and problems. It was really peaceful in that tunnel. I really didn't want to go back."

For Harry, that seemed to be the end of the story, or the end of anything worth telling. He stopped talking and I had to ask him, "What then?"

"What then? The next thing I knew I was back in bed. It must have been a while later, because I was awake, very groggy, but awake. My chest burned where they'd put the resuscitation paddles. Then, I guess it was some time later, but the next thing I remember my wife came in, and she bent down and kissed me. 'Honey,' she says, 'I'm so glad you're okay.'"

"Don't 'honey' me," I said. "What do you mean, calling Mom like that? You know how excited she gets, and with her heart. You could've killed her."

"You should've seen the look on my wife's face. She thought there was no way I could've known she called my mother, and she started to deny it, but I told her exactly what she said. I mean, I was *there,* I'd heard it, she had to admit it. She was crying. The only funny part of the whole thing was the look on her face. She just couldn't figure it out. It took me a long time before I made up with her. Don't misunderstand me, she's wonderful, greatest wife in the world. She's just not the calmest person, that's what I mean about her judgment.

That's why I have this feeling about doctors. You think I'm crazy, right?"

I assured him I did not think he was crazy. I suggested that he read Dr. Raymond Moody's book, *Life After Life,* which would help him validate the experience in his own mind and make him feel more comfortable with it.

I then questioned him about his relationship with his wife. After all, she had panicked because he meant so much to her, and perhaps he was being rather hard on her.

He seemed to become aware of that himself as he talked about her and their three children. Despite his tendency to criticize her, it was a good marriage, and he had a great deal to live for, a topic we then discussed at some length. When the figure in white had sent him back from the tunnel of light, he had felt dismay at the prospect of returning to life, but now, years later, he was a relatively happy human being, committed to staying alive and not killing himself "legitimately" with cigarettes.

It may seem strange, but the testimony of many people indicates that it is not uncommon for someone after a near-death experience to resent remaining alive. Such a person has seen the other side and would rather be there, at peace, than continue the often painful process of living. If I sense that a patient is contemplating an escape back into the tunnel, I offer immediate counsel on the possible ramifications of death, the loves ones left abandoned, the joys of life yet to be experienced, the sense of purpose being fulfilled that life offers, the obligation to experience all that the future still holds in store. I do not think God wants us to play God and resign from temporal existence at will. Like playing hookie from school, we might have to just start over.

In Harry's case, there was no difficulty; he was committed to living. With his permission, I called his wife and discussed the hospital incident. She confirmed the story of her phone call to his mother, and his inexplicable knowledge of exactly what she had done and said while he was still in the operating room. After that first long session and its unexpected detour, his resistance to hypnosis (to therapy in general and to me as a doctor) steadily dissipated. Perhaps because I had trusted him and taken his account of a near-death experience seriously, he in turn could begin to trust doctors. Perhaps, too, telling the story after all that time was a kind of emotional catharsis for him. In any event, the smoking therapy gradually achieved success.

More and more people are becoming aware of the NDE concept, and it is at last being considered worthy of serious study. This is thanks in large part to physicians such as Elizabeth Kubler-Ross, Raymond Moody, and Melvin Morse. The implications and the benefits of awareness are very interesting. Millions of people have undergone this experience, and many have believed they were losing their sanity. Many others have been afraid to disclose what they saw and heard lest others believe them mentally unbalanced.

I participated in an hour-long, call-in radio program on this topic, and we had phone calls from people who said they had been living with the secret of their near-death experience for ten or twenty years. They had burdened themselves with the conviction that they had suffered pathological hallucinations, and were extremely relieved to learn at last that what they had gone through had been an experience shared by countless others, in short a phenomenon that can be considered normal.

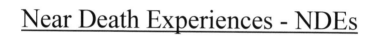

Near Death Experiences - NDEs

Chapter 18

A Reluctant Returner wants Out

"It's like we're born in a prison and don't know it until we get a glance of the world outside. Now I don't want to be in this prison anymore."

Sam

Some diseases are terminal, whether or not they are regarded as purely physical, and every physician faces the inevitability that the joy of healing will sooner or later be interrupted by a failure. I count Sam's case as one of those failures, one that I was helpless to prevent. A strictly orthodox diagnosis would have listed the cause as coronary disease, perhaps with a notation that deterioration was aggravated by constant smoking. That diagnosis would be accurate but incomplete. Severe as his smoking pattern was, it was a manifestation of a stronger drive, the wish to die to return to death.

He was forty-five years old, married, healthy enough in outward appearance, and cheerful in his manner, at least until he began to reveal his real problem to me. His relationship with his wife was mediocre, but they had a very young daughter, hardly more than a baby, and he loved the child and was happy in his role as a father. However, there were problems. He was not overtly suicidal nor did he suffer from chronic depression; or if he did, he hid it very well.

Both of Sam's parents had died of heart disease, and three years before he came to see me he had survived his first heart attack at the age of forty-two. More recently he had undergone a coronary artery bypass. During surgery he had suffered a cardiac arrest but had been quickly resuscitated, and his recuperation had been uneventful, except that he had resumed smoking. He thoroughly understood the danger, but seemed not to worry much about it. His efforts to quit had impressed the doctor as not especially sincere, and finally the cardiologist had referred him to me for help in breaking the addiction. Without question, smoking was going to kill him if he did not stop.

He readily admitted to me that before the bypass operation he had been smoking almost two packs of cigarettes a day, and now he was smoking two and a half or three packs a day. Other than that he seemed an intelligent man. From what he told me of his family, his work, his interests, and hobbies, it became clear that before his experience in the operating room, he had truly wanted to live. However, after the operation, his outlook on life had changed.

I pressed him to disclose what had changed his attitude since the operation. Finally he told me the more complete story.

While in cardiac arrest during the bypass surgery, he had undergone a near-death experience. Such experiences may leave survivors with less fear of death but a profound thankfulness to be returned to life. Sam's reaction, however, was otherwise. As he told me about it, he leaned forward in his chair as if to emphasize how earnest he was and how urgently he wanted me to believe and understand what had happened to him.

"Hell, Doctor," he said, "I might as well admit I'm here under false pretenses. Maybe after this the doctors and my wife will quit nagging me and leave me alone. Everybody goes on and on about how I'll live longer if I quit, and I'll die if I don't. So I'll die. That's fine with me, the sooner, the better."

I asked him why he was so eager to lose his life.

"Doctor," he said, "you can believe this or not, I don't care, but when my heart stopped on that operating table I got a good look at death. I saw the other side. It's hard to describe, but it was like I floated out of my body, up and out, and I was looking down at myself and the whole operating room scene. I can tell you everything the doctors and nurses were doing. Everything they were saying. You've probably read about this kind of thing. They say you go up into a tunnel of light. I've read about it and that's how they describe it, I mean people who've had that experience. Well, I'm here to tell you they're right. That's just how it was. Only nobody can adequately describe it. I can't tell you how peaceful it was, nobody can get that across so you'd understand unless it happened to you. It's a peace like no one can have on this side."

"But you came back," I said.

"Yeah," Sam replied, "but it wasn't that I wanted to. I saw somebody up there, in the tunnel, somebody or something I sort of had to obey."

"Whom did you see?

"I don't know. Just a figure in a white robe, pointing. He pointed and I saw Debbie, my little girl. I understood right away. I was going into this light and I knew if l kept going, Debbie would grow up without me. It was up to me, my decision, but I couldn't ignore what I saw. I didn't come back just because the doctors saved me. I came back because I made the decision. Now I can't help these feelings of regret, these feelings that I want to be back there again, forever, in that tunnel of light and the peaceful place."

"So now life looks different to you? Now it's not worth living out?"

"It's worse than that. I feel like we're born and raised in a prison and just don't know it. Then one day, chance puts me outside the prison. Why me? I don't know, but it happens; I get a peek outside the prison. What I see is this perfect peace. It's a kind of ecstasy. But I came back. I guess you could say I volunteered to come back, so here I am, but I'm also a little resentful. Only now all I do is wait. I'm just waiting for the light again. Sure, I'll feel guilty about leaving Debbie, but I can't help it. So tell me, why should I quit smoking?"

I tried hard to reason with him. I talked about the needs of his family, the many kinds of fulfillment to be found in life, the wonders of watching his child grow up, the crime of the thinly veiled, slow-motion suicide he was committing. But in the end it did no good. The patient left me, determined to return to the light sooner rather than later.

About six months later, Sam got his wish. Now Debbie will have to grow up without her daddy.

Chapter 19

"Just One more Thing…"

Joan was a healthy, lovely, gentle, former nun in her early 70s. She had come into my practice looking for a little counseling in getting through some current life situations. She was living alone on a small fixed income and was hoping to find some worthwhile pursuits as well as put to rest some old uncomfortable memories.

She had entered the convent as a teenager hoping to please God and her mother, and I suspect to do some sort of penance for some vague guilt which was not uncommon in her culture. After several decades she left her holy orders having become disenchanted with the dictatorial life-style, and feeling that somehow she had done her duty and served her time.

She was very open and honest in her counseling and quickly accomplished what she had come in for. The reason I talk about her here is to relate her story as it pertains to the other-worldly theme of this book.

Joan was born the last of eight children in a staunch Irish-Catholic family. Her father died of alcoholism shortly after Joan was born. Joan's mother was a fretful, angry person, and seemed to release much of her anger on her youngest child. As Joan grew through childhood, her mother's resentments never abated. Joan was told that she was a useless, unwanted, incompetent little ragamuffin. The little girl did everything she could to get her mother's approval, but it was a fool's errand.

Through childhood and adulthood, every night in her prayers she would ask that one day her mother would grow to love her. She fantasized that when her mother grew aged, she would be there to comfort and care for her. The mother lived into old age and eventually was hospitalized with heart failure. Joan would visit with her daily after work, and talk about the day as she combed her mother's hair. The mother still did not let go of her anger and bitterness. It seemed that after a lifetime of such an attitude, nothing was about to soften her feelings.

One day as she always did when Joan was ending her daily

visit, she said, "Goodnight mother. I hope you sleep well. I'll be by again tomorrow."

"Don't bother", the old woman said. "By tomorrow I'll be dead".

Joan was startled and shaken. Her mother had never said anything like that before. Joan tried to hide her anxiety as she replied with a smile, "Oh Mother don't talk like that. Sleep tight and I'll see you tomorrow afternoon."

Again her mother retorted, "Don't waste your time. This is good-bye. I'm tired of living. You won't have to see me again. Good night."

Joan left very upset. All night long and through the next day at work she anxiously awaited a phone call from the hospital saying that her mother had passed. But no call came.

After work she rushed back to the hospital and to her mother's room to find her sitting up in bed with a peaceful pleasant smile on her face. Joan was delighted and said, "See mother, I said you would be all right and that you wouldn't die."

"Oh no, I did die last night."

"What do you mean, Mother? You're here now alive, and you are looking lovelier than ever."

"But I did die last night. It was the strangest thing. I was lying here wishing for God to take me, and get me out of this miserable place. All of a sudden I was floating up to the ceiling and looking down on myself there in the bed. It felt so strange, but I was not scared at all. Then I continued floating up and I saw two figures up ahead. As I got closer I could see that one of them was you father and the other your brother Frank. Your father put out his hand and told me to stop. He said I had to go back, because there was something I still had to do. So I looked back at the bed and the next thing I know I was there in it again."

"That's amazing, Mother. I've never heard of such a thing. (This was in the early 1960s and Dr. Raymond Moody's very popular book on near death experiences was yet to be written.) What do you think Dad meant about what you still have to do?"

The old woman looked deeply and lovingly into Joan's eyes and said, "I love you".

Joan was beside herself with joy. There was her mother near the end of her life finally coming to realize and express that she loved her little girl. With tears in her eyes, Joan said, "I love you too, Mother".

Joan continued her daily visits, and two weeks later her mother went into coma. Still she dutifully visited each day and spoke to the comatose woman as she combed and stroked her thin gray hair. This was how she had always wished to be there at the end of her mother's life. Two weeks into the coma, as Joan was again telling her mother that she loved her, the woman opened her eyes, turned her head towards her daughter and gave her a loving, knowing smile. Joan was thrilled. She excitedly said to the patient in the other bed, "Look, my mother has woken up!" Then Joan looked right back at her mother's face only to find that the woman had breathed her last, but she still had that lovely smile.

Mind/Body Connection

Chapter 20

Comatose but Still Listening

"Thanks, but I'm not so sure I want to be here"

I met Mr. Miller during his last month of life; or perhaps I should say I encountered him, since he never spoke a word to me or anyone else during that entire time. I first saw him early on the first day of my one-month rotation in the intensive-care unit (I.C.U.) while I was a house officer (medical resident) at Johns Hopkins Hospital. He was a pleasant-looking man of fifty-five, and I was soon to learn that he had a lovely, devoted wife and equally devoted son. Although he had a healthy heart, liver, and kidneys, he had suffered a severe vascular disorder that had demanded surgery if he was not to be permanently incapacitated. It was a delicate and somewhat dangerous surgical procedure, but as far as medical science could determine, it had been entirely successful.

The only problem was that my new patient was in a coma. When the operation was finished, the effects of the anesthesia wore off, and when it was time for the patient to wake up, he simply did not. That had been a full thirty days before my month of duty in I.C.U. began. In our multimillion dollar I.C.U., he was hooked up to every appropriate monitoring device. But all the monitors in the world could neither help him open his eyes nor detect why he did not.

Every day, his wife and son drove fifty miles to the hospital and sat at his bedside for an hour or more, talking to him as if he could hear and respond. He gave no sign that he could hear them or was aware of their presence. The medical team at Johns Hopkins, acclaimed for their knowledge and experience, was baffled.

When we residents made our rounds each morning, the report was always close to the same: "blood pressure 125/82 and steady, heart rate 76 and regular, respirations 17 and unlabored." We would discuss the case, exchanging observations and reviewing the records. Sometimes our conversation turned to other matters before we left him. After all, Mr. Miller could not care or hear what we were talking about; he was in a deep coma. At times, the talk was about him and entirely serious, and at times the medical students present indulged in gallows humor, those nervous little jokes about suffering and death that relieve or cover up our uneasiness about the fragile, tenuous mortality surrounding us in a hospital setting.

I did not like those moments of humor at a comatose patient's bedside. I would remember the admonitions of some of my medical school mentors. They had cautioned that just because a person is in a coma and may show no response do not assume that the patient's senses are totally deactivated and that his mind does not absorb what he may very well be hearing. This hypothesis has been confirmed again and again by patients who, under hypnosis, minutely recall what they had heard while totally "unconscious" during surgery, including every word spoken by the surgeons, anesthetist, assistants, and nurses. My final encounter with Mr. Miller was one of those experiences that stand out in my mind as demonstrating how much more goes on in this process of life and death than we understand.

Day after day, I tended to the laconic man in bed No. 3, and my heart ached as I watched his family always dutifully and hopefully visiting and chatting. Always they asked the same question, although they knew the answer: "Any change since last night?" Then they would apologize for delaying me even a moment in my rounds and thank me for the attention I was giving to their loved one. I went into medicine to relieve suffering, and often I felt ineffectual, helpless, at times prolonging agony instead of relieving it.

Just once, during the third week of my rotation, we thought we saw some faint movement. I don't know if it was real or only wishful thinking. Maybe we were just grasping at straws, eager to see some glimmer of hope. It happened on the day when his son came to give him wonderful news. The patient in bed No.3 was a new grandfather. His first grandchild had been born, and mother and baby were fine!

There was no visible reaction, and the son leaned close to his father's face and repeated the announcement. Still there was no change of expression on Mr. Miller's face, but a single teardrop rolled from the outer corner of his left eye. Could this be a hint of approaching consciousness, of greater things to come, or perhaps simply a speck of dust had found its way under his eyelid? There was no further response and no way to elicit any. There was nothing more to do but to hope.

On the last evening of my thirty-day rotation, I wrote my detailed notes on my patients for the benefit of the resident who would be taking over my cases. It was a depressing evening. My closing notes on Mr. Miller looked very much like the closing notes the previous doctor had turned over to me a month before.

I sat there thinking about what Mrs. Miller had told me about her husband. He was a very proud, strong-willed man, accustomed to being independent and self-reliant. He had expressed anger at the disorder that had brought him into the hospital, and he was appalled by the probability that he would be at least partially dependent on the ministrations of others for a long time to come. The dangerous aspect of the surgical procedure had not dismayed him in the least, and he had approached it with an "all or nothing" attitude. "If I'm not going to be whole again," he had told her, "I won't want to be around!"

But he was not going to be whole again for some time if ever, at least in his interpretation of whole. The physicians had discussed the gravity of his case and the need for long-term recuperation on a number of occasions, perhaps during surgery and certainly at his bedside in the I.C.U. while he remained comatose. Had Mr. Miller been listening all that time, absorbing every word, slowly coming to a decision that he would not tolerate what he called "a vegetable existence?"

Essentially, he was a fighter, the kind of person who summons untapped reserves of strength to fight off death, and this could in some measure explain why his blood pressure, heart rate, respiration, all his life signs, had returned to and remained at such promising levels while he remained mysteriously comatose. But he was also a person who could face and deliberately choose death in favor of a dependent life.

The end of my one month rotation had come, and I decided I would have a serious, albeit one sided, discussion with my patient. I would disregard the possibility that he could not hear me. I felt he could, and I would try somehow one last time to bring him out of his coma. I pulled a chair up to his bedside and drew the curtain closed so that we could have a "private" chat. More honestly, I didn't want the nurses to see me having an intense, one-way discussion with a comatose patient.

"Mr. Miller, this is Dr. Jarmon. I've been taking care of you for the last month. The nursing staff and the other doctors have been doing all they can to get you better. I think you can pull out of this if you really want to, but I don't think you have been trying hard. Your family has been here every day, visiting you, and you know how much they care about you and want you home with them. Don't you think it's time you made a decision? We are doing everything that WE can, but it's up to you. You can work with us to help you get better or you can stop breaking your family's hearts by giving them false hope. It's a big decision, a terrible decision, so don't make it hastily, but I think you HAVE been making it, and you'll come out of this if you want to, but only if YOU want to."

I watched closely for the slightest sign of response.

There was none. I decided to continue.

"Mr. Miller, your condition hasn't changed at all in sixty days, and another doctor will be taking over your case tomorrow. So I would like to know your answer today. I'm going to see another patient now, but I'll be back in about fifteen minutes. I'm going to look for your decision then. I'm going to hope you've decided to come back to us. Now, try to blink if you've heard and understood what I've been telling you."

I looked at his face as closely as I ever studied anything in my life, wanting desperately to see him blink, or perhaps even open his eyes. I thought I saw an eyelid move, but I could not be sure. I drew open the curtain and proceeded to my other duties, wondering whether I had helped a fellow human being or had just performed a silly act.

Less than two minutes later, the alarm bells sounded on his vital function monitors. The nurse shouted to me that the man in bed No.3 was in cardiopulmonary arrest. We tried long and hard to resuscitate him to no avail. His soul had left his body. Mr. Miller had made his decision.

.

Chapter 21

Mother's Rainbow

Dealing with people's lives can be humbling and disquieting for all of us in the healing professions. So much faith is placed in us, and yet, there is so much we do not understand and cannot control. It is dismaying to realize that *every* human being inevitably must say or do things which have a direct effect on some other person's life or, in rarer instances, even on another person's acceptance of death. In the latter situation, our own attitudes concerning death, and the attitudes of fellow survivors, may also be deeply influenced.

Such occurrences are all the more unsettling when we are dealing with our own families. Still, there are lessons to be learned. I believe I learned something of lasting importance from an experience that took place long before I became a psychiatrist.

The year 1979 was terrible for my family. My mother-in-law was suffering from breast cancer. She came home from the hospital to die. The cancer had metastasized throughout her body, and there was no possibility of recovery. Moreover, the cancer in her bones made the slightest bodily movement excruciating.

I had studied and begun to practice hypnosis, and now I tried to ease her pain with hypnotic analgesia, but my initial attempts were disheartening. She could not at first accept my efforts without resistance. A devout Catholic who had raised her fifteen children in the faith, she gently, gratefully tolerated my attempts, but said in a voice that did not falter, "God must have a reason for my pain, and He alone can ease it."

Ultimately, I was able to give her some relief by having her transfer the image of her own pain to the image of Christ's suffering on the cross, couched in the format of prayer. I did not tell her that imagining a transfer of pain is a common technique in medical hypnosis. That would have done her no good, and I was thankful for any help I could provide.

That same week, my father entered the hospital with his fourth heart attack. My mother-in-law, weakening and in recurring pain, said she would pray for him to get well quickly. When I told Dad, he said, "Thank her for me, Bob, and tell her to concentrate on praying for herself. I'll get through this all right." A few days later, I dragged myself home after a twelve hour tour of night duty at a hospital to learn that my father had just died.

My mother-in-law was a woman of exceptionally strong constitution, but over the next two months her condition continued to deteriorate. Finally, she became too weak even to sip liquids. The time had come for the doctors and family to make a painful decision. Her agony would not be allowed to be prolonged by administering intravenous fluids. She slipped into a coma and there were no further attempts at therapy.

The family gathered from distant points, and a death watch began. For two days, her blood pressure hovered at 40 palpable, with labored breathing. Her strength had always been beautiful, and it had not been squandered. She was clinging to her painful existence with every fiber of her tormented being. The children were exhausted. At such a time there is no shame in wishing or praying for the end to come.

Remembering my previous observations of a comatose patient at the hospital, I gathered the family to her bedside and told them I believed the end was close. "If there's anything you want to say to Mother, I think you should tell her now. She's too weak to answer, but I believe she can still hear you." For those left behind, it can be very important to say a few last words to express their love and make their peace.

Several members of the family spoke their final words to her, and when all who wished to speak had done so I took her hand. "It's all right, Mother," I said, "it's all right for you to go now." Her pale, withered lips seemed to tighten with resolve and her head turned slightly, as if in defiance of death.

One of her sons, Gregory, gently took her other hand and spoke to her again. "It's okay, Mother. We all love you, and we release you. You've done your work." Her daughter Margaret softly added a few words, confirming what Gregory had said.

"You can go to your rest now, Mother," I said. "We all love you, and we'll be with you soon enough."

With that, her breathing stopped. Someone had left the

television set on in the next room, and her favorite movie, *The Wizard of Oz,* was being aired. At the moment she died, we could hear the melody of her favorite song, "Over the Rainbow."

The next day was cold and drab. Several of us were standing in the living room, talking only intermittently. A moment came when there was complete silence as we faced the large picture window and gazed out over the dark ocean. Then, one by one, we became aware of a gentle light brightening the room. Forming an arc over the sky was an enormous rainbow, and above and behind it, a secondary one. None of us could speak. At last, as the primary rainbow began to shift and fade, one of the children softly voiced the thought that had taken hold of all of us.

"It's Mother. She's made it over. She's telling us it's okay to be at peace."

Still spellbound, we nodded our heads.

Two days later, my wife Mary was clearing away medications and various other items on Mother's nightstand. Onto the floor fell that week's missalette, a collection of devotions which the priest had left for her a few days earlier. On its cover was a rainbow and the words, "The bow in the sky shalt be thy covenant."

Many years have passed, and still my voice falters when I tell people this story. Mary's mother provided me with a lesson about the healing arts which I had missed in my medical training and experience. It was another example that beyond the measurable there exists a mind-body-spirit connection that we can be open to, though not fully understand.

Chapter 22

Repressed Memories Validated, and
Strange Lesions Healed

Nancy was a single, pleasant looking 40 year old social worker who had come into therapy for a sporadic, generalized anxiety. At times the anxiety flare ups would be associated with rectal irritation and bleeding. She had seen a proctologist for this and had been treated with topical steroids to control these inflammations of unknown cause. Nancy was intelligent, dedicated, and well liked at work. She had intimacy problems with men, which was why she had never married. We did some talk therapy and tried to analyze the source of her discomfort, but failed to find anything definitive. Because of her discomfort with men, we were never able to achieve a good hypnotic trance to try and find the source of her problems. I had suggested that she try working with a female therapist, but she declined saying that she believed ultimately she would allow herself to be hypnotized. There are hypnotic techniques for essentially tricking someone into hypnosis, but in Nancy's case I felt that if it failed, she would lose what trust she had in me.

One day while reviewing her family relationships again, I asked if there were some family history of emotional problems. She hesitated and then said, "Hadn't I told you about my Uncle Billy?"

"No. I don't recall that you did and I don't see anything in my notes about it".

"Oh, I thought I had".

"Tell me about him. What was his problem and how were you related to him?"

"Uncle Billy was a child molester. In fact he went to prison for several years. He was my father's brother"

"What else do you know about him, and what was he like?"

"He was pretty much a drifter. He worked as a clown and also a salesman. He was always the life of the party. Uncle Billy was very gregarious and charismatic. In hindsight, I suppose he had the personality of a con artist. He certainly conned a lot of people into thinking he was something that he was not. In fact some of his victims were my cousins."

All of a sudden this patient's case was looking like it might have a distinct direction.

I said, "How much time did you spend with Uncle Billy?"

"He lived with us for about six months when I was four years old. I don't remember much if anything about it, though".

"What did your parents think of him?"

Dad felt sorry for him, which was why he let Uncle Billy stay with us for a while. Mother thought he was entertaining and appreciated that he could baby sit for me when they went to work."

"Did they know at the time that he was a child molester?"

"Oh no, that only came out years later. I was in college by then. While in prison he had a sort of *awakening* and made an effort to contact all the children he had molested and asked for their forgiveness."

"Did he ever contact you?"

"No, why would he? I don't remember him ever doing anything to me."

At this point I needed to be especially cautious. She had no memories of being abused and she may not have been. But more often than not, the victims of childhood abuse have blocked out the memories from their conscious mind. And even if we could do hypnotic regression, it is too easy to implant false memories so that later the patient believes that incest occurred. It was also troubling that the patient had essentially no conscious memories of being with her uncle though he spent half a year with her. I decided to ask questions which were more tangential.

"Tell me some more about him. Does your uncle remind you of anyone?"

"Yes, in fact he reminds me very much of my supervisor, Fred, whom by the way I cannot stand."

As it happened I knew her supervisor through my work. He

was a very gregarious and well-liked man.

"Why do you think you don't like Fred?"

"I don't know. I just don't. In fact whenever I have to see him in his office, I seem to get a flare-up of my rectal problem. Everyone else seems to adore him and think he's the life of the party. I just hate being in his presence."

"Nancy, I certainly do not want to put ideas into your head, but listen to what you have just been telling me. You have dealt with people from troubled childhoods. What would you think if someone were relating this story to you, the way you have been telling it to me?"

She sat there silent and contemplative for a minute or two. Then she said, "I'm afraid I see where this might be going."

"You said your uncle had been making efforts to contact his victims and ask their forgiveness. This sounds as if it could be one of those rare but fortuitous opportunities to get to the truth directly from the source. What do you think?"

Nancy sat there silent again. Then she said, "I know how to get in touch with him. Is it okay if I think about this, and we can discuss it some more next week?"

"Of course you can."

The following week Nancy came into the office smiling and excited. She had a voice recorder in her hand. "I thought about everything we had discussed, and I decided to bite the bullet and go for it. I called my uncle and recorded the telephone conversation so that I could listen to it again and also bring it to you for your opinion."

In essence their conversation went like this. Nancy called him and asked how he was doing, and mentioned that she had been in therapy and discussing her childhood. Very politely she asked him if there was any information he could offer that might help her understand her anxieties. He totally opened up to her, answered all of her questions, and asked for forgiveness for sexually abusing her when she was 4 years old. At her request he described the nature of the abuse which included anal intercourse. As I listened to the tape I felt that he was being very forthright. She said that she did forgive him, and that act of hers became part of her healing.

Nancy and I discussed the abuse, her lifelong anxieties, and her rectal pathology. She easily then connected the dots between her uncle's personality, that of her boss, and her physical problem.

I asked if she would like to do some hypnosis and put this all to rest. She enthusiastically said yes.

I found it very common in cases of abuse that once the one individual culprit is identified, in this case a male, it opens the door for the victim to be able to let the rest of the male population off the hook. She knows whom to be afraid of. In a sense it is treating a phobia by uncovering the repressed offending incident.

Like a storybook ending, we did the hypnosis, she saw that it was her uncle who violated her, she would never again let herself be vulnerable to him, and she had no need to fear her supervisor. Her anxieties left as did her rectal bleeding. With that she soon finished therapy. We kept in touch for two more years and there were no recurrences as she steadily became more comfortable with men.

Some people do not believe in repressed memories. They think that if something that bad really happens, it would be impossible to forget. They are wrong. When something very bad happens, yes we remember it. But when something absolutely horrendous takes place, we repress it. It's our mind's way of protecting us. The problem is that though the memory is hiding, the emotion connected with it lingers but with no place to assign it. The cure is to locate the source, tie the appropriate emotion to it, and then relegate it to history as you move forward.

The Watchers - Help from Beyond

Chapter 23

The Old Fireman

Tom is a professional firefighter. His father is also a career fireman, as was Tom's grandfather. Professional firefighters are an interesting group. For the most part they are highly trained, physically fit, courageous, tough, and hardened by experience as well as training. They are extremely loyal to one another. The kind of man who is attracted to such a career is seldom the kind who is quick to seek a psychiatrist, and would say, "You have to be crazy to do that". Fortunately, many metropolitan fire departments have come to regard psychiatric counseling as an intrinsic part of health care, but it was not on orders from his department that Torn first carne to see me.

He had been struggling with post-traumatic stress disorder after a terrible fire had taken the lives of six of his comrades. He was experiencing paranoid delusions and severe nightmares. An intelligent and willing patient, he improved with surprising speed under short-term psychotherapy which included clinical hypnosis. After two months, he was functioning normally, a happy and well-adjusted man again. His therapy complete, I didn't hear from him again for about two years. Then I received a somewhat puzzling phone call.

"How are you doing?" I asked. "Have any problems resurfaced from that fire?"

"Oh no, nothing like that," Tom replied. "It's something else, and this time you're going to think I'm really going crazy. Can I come see you? I don't want to tell you over the phone. It's a long story."

When he arrived at my office, he seemed uncharacteristically nervous. Something seemed to have shaken him. For a few minutes he talked about everything except the purpose of his visit. Most people are reluctant to share their innermost feelings and even more reluctant to divulge bizarre experiences. They fear that a normal, intelligent person will not believe what they have to tell, which is why I kept a crystal ball on my desk. I point to it and say, "Any psychiatrist who keeps a crystal ball around like medical equipment is a shrink you can share *any* story with". They usually smile or laugh, and more often than not they open up.

Tom began to tell me his story, and it indeed had some bizarre aspects. About two months previously, his fire company had been called to a warehouse fire on a dark, cloudy night. The power was out in the building, and they had no layout of the warehouse to help them find their way through. The smoke was so thick that their lighting equipment was of no use inside the structure.

"Did you ever drive through a thick fog?" Tom asked me. "The headlights shine against a fog that looks like a wall and you can't see past it. It was like that, only much worse. Our lights just didn't help."

A group of men entered the ground floor groping through the smoke. Tom then lost radio contact with them. In the noise and confusion, Tom went in after them, alone, looking for his men and dragging a hose line so that they would be able to follow it back out. He found that four men had fallen through a large trap door on the ground floor, and some stored appliances had fallen through the burning floor, landing on them. By that time, Tom's oxygen tank was almost empty, and he went out again to get more manpower and a fresh oxygen tank.

He and a couple of others managed to bring out three of the fallen men, but could not budge the fourth. He was unconscious, pinned under a large freezer. They could not lift the freezer and their oxygen was again almost gone. Moreover, the unconscious firefighter was such a large man that they would not be able to maneuver him up through the trap opening, which was now partially blocked by fallen timbers and boxes. As the officer in charge, Tom made the toughest decision a firefighter has to face. He ordered his men to abandon the fallen firefighter and to get out while they could still leave under their own power. He did not think the injured man could hear him, but he told him they would return and get him out.

He immediately reported to his battalion chief who agreed it would be useless to go back in the same way and suggested going in through a hatch that led to the basement. Torn went in again, taking with him the only two men available, a rookie and an older fire man near retirement. The inexperienced young man was obviously fearful as he tried to grope through the blinding smoke, but they were not going to leave a fallen comrade to die. Courage is not the absence of fear but the ability to overcome it.

"Sometimes," Tom told me, "I don't know what to do next in a situation like that, and that's the worst part of it. I'm a pro. I should always know what to do. You know what I'm trying to say?"

All too well, I thought, and I nodded as he continued.

"At times like that, maybe it sounds odd, but I ask my grandfather for help. 'Poppy', I say, 'what do I do now?' He died when I was nine, but even then I thought he was the greatest fireman who ever lived. So I ask him, and would you believe I always get an answer? It happened again this time. I could hear him say, 'Put out your right hand, Tommy. There's a masonry wall. Follow it. Just follow it as far as it goes.' So I reached out, and there was the wall. I got to the end of it, and here's the really weird part. It was still dark in there and smoky, but as God is my witness I saw Bill, the guy who was trapped, and he was glowing. About twenty feet away from me! I could even see he'd vomited. He was glowing in some kind of white light, and there was a yellow glow right over his head. I thought, my God, he's dying and his soul is leaving his body! The two guys with me, they didn't see a thing, only I did."

Tom guided the others to where Bill lay, and this time they managed to lift the freezer away. But by that time their oxygen was depleted. Then Tom heard his grandfather speak again: "It's time to go, Tommy." He could not be sure Bill was alive; and if he were, Tom feared he would die if they left him again. But he heard his grandfather repeat, "Tommy, it's time to go."

He and the two other rescuers found their way out, following the hose they had laid down. Five fresh rescuers then went in the same way and with the freezer no longer pinning Bill, they were quickly able to get him out. By the time he reached the hospital, he had regained consciousness.

"They tell me he'll probably be as good as new," Tom said.

"That's a wonderful story," I said. "Bill owes his life to you. But I don't understand what's troubling you. You and the others saved his life."

"It's a couple of things, Doc. First of all, what if he'd died? I mean, I left him twice and he could have died. What about the other part, I mean about his soul? I saw it. Either I saw it or I'm going crazy. What about hearing Poppy, my grandfather? How do I explain that?"

Sometimes psychiatry and spirituality walk the same path. I believe Tom did see Bill's spirit or soul, whatever you choose to call it, and I told him so. I understood, too, about the advice his grandfather gives him in times of need. I told him that as well, and eventually persuaded him to accept it as a gift of the most wonderful kind.

I have a similar feeling about my own father and how he helps me in my work. Dad was a marvelous counselor, though not by vocation. When I was a teenager, some of my friends liked to come to my house as much to talk with him as to do things with me. Ever since he passed away in 1979, when I need sound advice I have only to ask: what would Dad tell me to do? I cannot say I *hear* him in a physical sense, as Tom hears his grandfather, but I see no reason why that must be essential in every case. An appropriate answer never fails to occur to me. Is it my father's spirit communicating with me? Or is it just that I came to know his approach to problems so well that by "asking" him I detach myself from the problem and think of an answer of he would have provided?

I gave Tom some reading matter about near-death experiences and related phenomena. He appeared to come to peace with that and needed no other therapy. He also tells me that he considers himself lucky to have found a doctor who keeps a crystal ball.

****

A relationship between a grandparent and a grandchild often provides special functions in society. For the grandparent it is a way to continue to be useful and have a sense of purpose, and the better if the grandparent is held in awe and loved for the knowledge, protection, and attention given. It also provides a way for the older generation to see that there will be a future.

For the grandchild the grandparent can be a source of comfort, protection and good counsel, at times a buffer and champion for the child when there is conflict with a parent. This special bond can extend after death as related in the above story.

I had another patient whose life was saved by her dead grandfather. She was driving around a sharp bend in the road on a dark, rainy night when suddenly her grandfather appeared in front of her car. He had died a few years before, and they had been very close. As soon as she saw him she steered the car off to the side of the road, up onto the shoulder, then slammed on the brakes. Just as she stopped an out of control truck swung around the curve from the opposite direction and into the lane she had been on. If she had not swerved to avoid her grandfather, she probably would have been killed.

Chapter 24

Fatherly Advice from the Departed

Bill and Cathy have been good friends of ours for many years. We share the same sort of appreciation for many of life's values concerning family and the joys of living, although Bill has always been skeptical about spiritual concepts, especially theories about an afterlife. He always had a view of life which he described as pragmatic. However, now he knows now that there can be more than one kind of reality and that all of us must sometime wonder what is or is not real.

Whereas Bill saw himself a realist, Cathy tends to be meditative. She has had spiritual experiences while meditating and has always accepted that there is more to the cosmos than we can see or explain.

Even after Bill underwent an experience that defied all his mechanistic views, he was reluctant (which sometimes means afraid) to accept what he could not explain. Cathy helped him begin to achieve acceptance, and I like to think I did, too.

Until 1990 Bill held a high-level managerial position with a Fortune 500 company, but during that time of severe economic recession he was furloughed and soon realized the furlough would be permanent. He had lost his job, and being unaccustomed to failure he did not take it well. Unable to accept the very idea that he had been dismissed, he had difficulty seeking a new managerial position.

Our social visits and dinner-table talks did not help.

During the Vietnam War, he had been a Marine Corps officer, and he had thrived on finding pragmatic solutions to tactical problems. In civilian life, he had savored the same responsibility of command, the same logical approach to business problems. When the conversation turned to spiritual matters, he could not help smirking just a little. "Bob, you're a great friend and I'm sure you're a great 'shrink,' but people have enough troubles without your filling their heads with this spirit stuff. Maybe they like to hear about the spirit world from some gypsy lady in a carnival, but not from the doctor. You'd better be careful or they'll think you're the one who should be on the couch."

It was good-natured teasing, and I was not about to seriously argue the point with him. There was, after all, no way that I could shake the foundations of his beliefs, nor did I wish to. Beneath his gentle mocking, he respected my right to my beliefs, and I respected his. But his were about to be shaken by something more powerful than any arguments I could have made.

After being out of work for over a year, Bill was finally contacted by a corporation in need of his managerial skills. But the good news was mixed with bad. He would have to move from New Jersey to the Midwest. He had been born and raised at the Jersey Shore, as I was, and I could appreciate his attachment to his home grounds. In his case, it was especially strong. He still owned a beachfront summer cottage where he had spent childhood vacations, and his emotional attachment to it was so intense that he had told Cathy he would sell their home if finances forced a sale, rather than sacrifice their summer place.

There were no jobs available where the summer house was located, nor was the school system as good as the schools where he and Cathy and their children lived. But such factors failed to move him; he could not bear the prospect of losing the cottage. Nevertheless, he was going to have to accept the job in the Midwest. To make matters worse, he would have to be there alone for the time being, leaving Cathy and the children in New Jersey until he could be sure the new job was a good fit.

As he prepared to leave, he was feeling severe pangs of separation. On the night before his departure, in a marked state of depression, he told his wife that he was going to spend one last night alone in the cottage. It was the next morning that, unnerved, he called and told me what had happened that night.

Bill had decided to sleep in his parents' old bedroom. His mother had died two years previously and his father twenty years before that. He was not mourning, but had recently thought fleetingly about his father and their relationship. He had always admired his father and longed to be closer to him, but the father had been somewhat preoccupied with a very demanding job and had seemed to have little time for his son.

As Bill told me about his night in the cottage, he occasionally sobbed and his voice revealed intense emotion, a side of him he never showed until now. "Bob," he said, "I… I don't know how to tell you this. I hope I'm not going crazy. Cathy says I should just accept it, it's perfectly normal. *Normal*, she says! Maybe she can accept it, I can't."

I tried to calm him and when his voice was more controlled I asked him to tell me exactly what had happened.

"Something very weird," he said. At least, I *think* it happened. I tried to tell myself it was a dream. Maybe it was. But it was real. I mean it was as real as this right now, Cathy *sitting* here, me talking to you. You know I never believed this soul stuff, only now I don't know what I believe. I don't even know what I feel. Bob, my father talked to me last night. I woke up in my parents' bed and there he was, standing there, looking at me. He looked fine. Really my God, I thought he was alive. Not like some ghost in a movie. He seemed altogether solid and real. It was pitch-black and I could see him plain as day. Bob, he *talked* to me. Even for you this has to be a new one. Am I going nuts?"

I reassured him and he seemed very relieved to hear that such accounts were not unheard of or new to me. I believed him; and no, he was not losing his mind.

He came over to talk some more about the strange experience. The room had been totally dark, black, and he could not understand how he could have seen anything at all. He had tried again and again to persuade himself that it had been a vivid dream. After his father or whatever the vision was had vanished, he got out of bed to see if any light was corning through the blinds. He stumbled as he groped toward the window because it was so dark.

Again I calmed him, and tried to give him a brief lesson about the concept of guiding spirits. I told him that it was perfectly all right to believe his father had talked to him and he probably had. I asked him what his father said.

"I actually heard his voice. He told me, 'Billy, it's time to stop worrying and get on with what you have to do. Cathy loves you, the kids love you. Everything will work out. I didn't spend enough time with you, I didn't tell you some of the things you need to understand. But you'll never be alone. Now you have to take a chance; grab the opportunity. It's going to be fine.' Maybe he said more, I'm not sure. But I can still hear him and that's what I remember. Then he was gone."

Bill had not gone back to sleep for fear the vision would return. He asked me if I thought it would. I said I could only guess. I shared with him accounts of similar experiences, stories he would never have believed until now. Then I said I did not think his father would return again soon.

"You needed him," I said. "You needed his visit, his encouragement, and you got it. I'd love to have a visit from my father. His body died fourteen years ago, but I know he'd be there for me if I needed him. But suppose your father does appear again. There's no reason to be afraid of that; he'll be there to help you. Think of all the things you might want to ask him if he comes again. Then, if he does, you'll welcome the experience. There's nothing to dread."

"Yes," Bill said, "I think I can do that. You know, Bob, I had a very odd feeling when I left the cottage. I can't explain it, but for the first time in my life that little house was just a house, like any other cottage in the neighborhood. It's just a place where people lived for a while, where other people might live later. I'm beginning to believe it really was my father's ghost I saw, and that he gave me something else other than just what he said about taking a chance and counting on Cathy and the kids. It was like being released from some kind of attachment I didn't need any more. That cottage no longer has some kind of hold over me. I can truly say I can leave it now without any regrets.

Later that same week, Bill moved alone to the Midwest to begin his new job. After he was settled and was handling the position well, Cathy flew out and together they went house hunting. They obtained a mortgage approval and were about to buy a home out there and sell their New Jersey home when Bill's boss told him he had earned a promotion and would be needed back in the headquarters offices, close to the Jersey Shore. He and Cathy kept their home, and their security seemed assured. It was as if a higher power had been testing Bill's faith and resolve.

The question remains: what was Bill's vision? Was it his

father's spirit? These guiding souls, or whatever you wish to call them, seem to me to be like personal trainers or guides who help us negotiate the obstacle course of our lives. In a brief single lifetime, each of us has to conquer fear, prejudice, greed, separations, isolation, and other adversities to happiness and peace. Whatever we have not learned by the time we die, we may come back to work on at a future time. But for the present, an angel or guide, trainer or even ghost may help us surmount our obstacles. The spirit may appear when needed and whisper what we need to know.

As children, most of us were told there are no such things as ghosts. Later in life some of us learned that very possibly they do exist. There are, of course, many famous stories of ghosts, such as Abraham Lincoln's repeated appearances in the White House. Lacking definitive proof, we decide for ourselves what to believe.

All of the accounts of ghosts that I have heard or read seem to share a common theme: that the deceased subject died with some mission unresolved, some purpose unfulfilled, or some future task to be completed. It is as if the spirit is duty bound not to depart permanently until its tasks are finished. I have included the subject of ghosts in this book because it comes up from time to time with patients. It is an emotionally charged issue which should be addressed. Sometimes a patient who recounts a ghostly experience may be out of touch with reality. But I have known a number of fairly well-adjusted people who are quite certain they have encountered ghosts. Many such apparitions may be manifestations of post-traumatic stress disorder (PTSD), which is marked residual emotional distress resulting from a tremendously disturbing event. But other cases are not so easily explained, especially when the observer has no prior knowledge of or emotional connection to the deceased and has no clinical symptoms of emotional dysfunction.

The science of physics tells us that energy is neither created nor destroyed but only changes form. What then becomes of psychic energy, spirit energy, when the body it inhabits ceases its life process? Is this energy the mysterious thing we call the soul, and can it take the form of a spirit, a ghost? Could this be akin to what physicists refer to as plasma, the fourth state of matter (the first three states being "solid, liquid, and gas") which is part energy, part matter (plasma is defined as a highly ionized gas containing an approximately equal number of positive ions and electrons)? Or perhaps we should simply view these apparitions as manifestations of a fifth state of matter and proceed to research the laws of nature which govern their behavior.

POSTSCRIPT

After some deliberation, Bill and his wife decided to not move back to New Jersey. He was enjoying his new job, and the children were enjoying the prospect of their new surroundings. Perhaps his father's message that everything would work out well and there was no need for concern, was becoming manifest.

As Easter of 1995 approached, Bill and his family were feeling very much at home in Oklahoma. Some government officials were coming into town for a meeting with representatives from his company. Bill's boss told him to call and book a meeting room at the Murrah facility in Oklahoma City. As Bill was in the process of requesting the meeting room, he thought otherwise and against his bosses wishes, arranged for a different venue, miles away.

As Bill, his boss, and the visiting officials were sitting down to meet, they heard a large distant explosion and felt a tremendous shaking. It was Wednesday, April 19, 1995 and the Alfred P. Murrah Federal Building had just been bombed.

Chapter 25

Father's help from above... and to the right

In 1972 I was a medical student in Newark, NJ. I was working in an emergency room and Dad was asking me about my day. I told him how I had just treated two gunshot wound victims. One was a police officer and the other was the man who had shot him. In the E.R. we treated all people equally regardless of how or why they came in.

That's when my father told me one of the few stories he shared about the war. He had been an assistant battalion surgeon in the Medical Administrative Corps (M.A.C.), and active in the Battle of the Huertgen Forest. In November 1944 a series of temporary truces were called over three days so that both sides could care for and remove their wounded from the field. It was a small area, probably less than an acre. After evacuating the wounded, the two sides would go back to trying to kill each other. Dad told me how both the German and the American medics cared for all of the injured soldiers regardless of uniform. He was the triage officer directing the evacuation of the wounded when a German medic gave him his *Weimarcht* (German Army) field medical kit as a token, and Dad gave the kit to me.

Sixty-nine years later, for my 70th birthday, I went to Germany and hired a local guide to take me to the Kall Trail a few miles southeast of Aachen, to where the incident had taken place. I learned that while such truces were not uncommon during our Civil War, this was the only such recorded incident in all of WW II. Over 200 G.I.s were evacuated. I then also discovered that a picture of the event, "A Time for Healing", had been painted by an army artist assigned to the camouflage unit. If my father knew about the picture he never told me.

I read that the picture was on display at the 28th Infantry Division headquarters in Harrisburg, Pa. When I called about making the 3 hour car ride out to see it I was delighted to learn that there had been a limited number of signed prints made, some additionally signed by some of the medics who were there, and that after all these decades there were four prints left. I bought two, one for myself and one for my brother. Jack was delighted with the gift and I told him the story behind it. He had not been aware of Dad's experience at the Kall Trail nor of the existence of the picture.

The day after Jack received my gift he contacted me to say that he had just been invited to the Army War College to speak about his recently published book, "The New Era in U.S. National Security" and invited me to come as his guest and support him. The army would video tape his talk and circulate it through the armed forces and the public. I was very happy for him and looked forward to the trip. I thought, however, that my kid brother could use a lot more support than just my presence in the audience. I said some silent prayers, "Dad, if you're still out there watching over us, now would be a great time to step up to the plate, give Jack a hand, and let him know he's not alone."

Jack gave a terrific presentation and showed a very confident presence that I had never before observed in him. He told me afterwards that he had felt that our father was up there with him, giving him all the support that he needed. What was most strange and wonderful was that the night before, when Jack arrived at Camp Carlisle and checked into his room on the base, there on the wall by his bed was a print he recognized, "A Time for Healing". The scene depicts several U.S. and German soldiers and corpsmen. In center left is one lone American officer with a clipboard, triaging the wounded. He is looking down and to his right where Jack's bed was. That officer was our father.

"A Time for Healing", Robert M. Nisley, U.S. Army

Spirit Attachment

Chapter 26

It's Awfully Crowded in Here

A book that discusses the soul, or spirit, in the context of psychotherapy needs to include at least some comment about the concept of spirit attachment and what is known as spirit releasement therapy. This should probably begin with a clarification of nomenclature, which scrupulously avoids the terms *possession* and *exorcism,* although some therapists refer to "clinical de-possession" as a synonym for releasement.

Dr. William Baldwin, a prominent advocate of this therapeutic modality, has explained the choice of terminology in an audiocassette and in his book, *Regression Therapy, Spirit Releasement Therapy.* "The entire concept of spirit interference or attachment," he explains, "met with superstitious resistance to the ominous specter of demonic possession and exorcism as depicted in the movie *The Exorcist.* The title or designation for the work needed to be descriptive, inclusive, and accurate, yet distinctly different from and not suggestive of demonic spirit possession or the stylized religious rituals of classic exorcism."[6]

Thus, the phenomenon is designated "attachment" rather than "possession." The word *release,* as Dr. Baldwin notes, carries the essence of the therapy, and adding the suffix *"ment"* indicates the *process* of releasing.

Now for the harder questions: What (as precisely stated as possible) do the terms denote and is there any validity to the concept?

The theory begins with the tenet that each of us has a soul, or spirit, and when the body dies the spirit must go somewhere. If this transition occurs without impediments, the soul departs into the tunnel of light and toward the "oneness," but there are other possibilities. The spirit may remain earthbound.

---

[6] William Baldwin, *Regression Therapy, Spirit Releasement Therapy,* pp. 157- 158.

Some theorize that a soul may not initially leave the earth plane if it perceives that its body has not died; or it may refuse to proceed into the tunnel of light because it feels it has an unfinished task on earth or feels unworthy or even afraid of returning to the "oneness." Or it may feel a special connection or affinity with a living person, stemming from any emotion from love to hate. Alternatively the soul of a drug addict or alcoholic may continue to yearn for drugs or liquor and may seek to invade a living person so as to continue to experience the addiction. There are also those who believe that an earthbound soul sometimes feels an overwhelming affinity for a place and its past associations, rather than for a living person; hence, an explanation of ghosts and haunted houses, again a famous example being Abraham Lincoln's ghost in the White House.

Can any of these things be possible? Logic indicates that there may never be a definitive answer concerning the reality of such phenomena, but logic also indicates the possibility, however bizarre it may seem. Records and reports suggest that more than eight million Americans have had a near-death experience in which the soul left the body and returned. If the soul can do that, why can it not also, under certain circumstances, turn back from the tunnel and enter another person's being? According to Dr. Baldwin, who has made a study of the subject, "in ninety percent of societies worldwide, there are records of possession-like phenomena".[7] He also cites "extensive clinical evidence which indicates that discarnate beings, the spirits of deceased humans, can influence living people by forming some sort of connection and causing physical and emotional problems."[8]

He goes on to say that such a disembodied consciousness, or spirit, having merged somehow with the subconscious mind of its living host, is like an invisible parasite, exerting some degree of control over the host's mind and, in some instances, the body as well. A great many people may be parasitized in this way, but most are unaware of the invasion, of the presence of one or more

---

[7] Ibid., p. 9.

[8] Ibid., p. 9.

spirits in addition to their own. They are aware only of physical or mental symptoms of unknown cause, such as sudden, inexplicable impulses or behavior. For that matter, an attached spirit may in some cases be present without producing noticeable symptoms. The unawareness (even when symptoms are manifest) is, according to Baldwin, a major factor in the reluctance to accept the concept of "discarnate interference."

So, too, is the belief that any such symptoms stem from more familiar machinations of the psyche. One clinician may suspect that chronic fatigue is caused by the stress and energy drain of spirit attachment, while others diagnose it as the result of known physical or emotional disorders. Total attachment and dominance by the infiltrating spirit, a "take-over" of the host, might cause a drastic personality change, a suppression of the original personality, but so can more common dysfunctions and illnesses.

Thus, many therapists would ascribe the symptoms of spirit attachment to a schizoid syndrome or to a multiple-personality disorder, which causes a person at times to speak and behave in a manner entirely different from his or her normal pattern.

On the other hand, this type of familiar, easier to accept diagnosis can be frustrated by an afflicted person who hears voices (internal or external) or sees images of unknown faces or figures, or reveals other such symptoms, *but exhibits no other psychotic symptoms or behavior.* If this is "simply" hallucination, what causes it, and are we so knowledgeable that we can state categorically that spirit attachment is not the explanation?

My personal experience with this therapy is very limited. However it may be worthwhile to tell you about a patient I helped to take into this *terra incognita* when other therapeutic stratagems had failed to work.

My patient was Chris, a hard-working family man in his late thirties who had decided to find out whether psychotherapy could relieve his nebulous feelings of anxiety and self-doubts as well as mounting marital discord. During several months of therapy, we uncovered quite a few repressed memories. He remembered that during his childhood he had been sexually abused by other boys, and he remembered two near-death experiences that his conscious mind had blocked out. In the course of working through those near-death experiences, he was able to comprehend and thus shed anxieties that amounted to mild phobias. He seemed to be making good progress when we hit an odd and unexpected barrier, an unnamed something present in his mind that prevented further headway. One day as I began to counsel him, he said, "Wait, I have to tell you about this thing I feel. There's something in the middle of my head that needs to come out."

Before the time came for his next appointment, he called me. He had become increasingly troubled about the thing he perceived inside his head, and now he added that it was exerting some kind of control over him. He had an uneasy sense that it was something evil.

For years, he had listened to his parish priests warning parishioners about the dangers of the forces of evil, and now Chris was beginning to feel that this evil was in no way allegorical but an actual, palpable force that had somehow invaded his being. Given the litany of traumas he had endured in childhood, he wondered if during one of those times of weakness and suffering something evil had seized the opportunity to infiltrate his body and mind.

I had never so much as considered the possibility that an emotional disturbance could be caused by a resident spirit, evil or otherwise. A cancer patient weakened by chemotherapy is at risk of becoming a host for pathological bacteria, but bacteria are, after all, *physical* entities. Physicians are not inclined to regard intangible entities in the same way, and it had never occurred to me that a weak state of body, mind, or spirit could be similarly vulnerable to attack and infiltration by uninvited spirits.

Since Chris viewed the "forces of evil" in the light of his church's teachings, I suggested that he talk to his priest about his concern. He told the priest he was afraid that the devil or one of his minions, had taken hold of him; that perhaps during one of those times when he had been near death or wishing he were dead, a hostile spirit had attached itself to his soul. He told the priest he had never taken the warnings from the pulpit literally, but now he did and wanted to know how to combat the evil presence. (In the Bible there are accounts of men possessed by "unclean spirits," and Christ directs those spirits to leave their hosts. In Mark, Chapter One, he releases such a spirit from a man in Capernaum. In Mark, Chapter Five, Christ releases multiple spirits which are afflicting a man from Gerasene, and thereby heals him. In 1993, Pope John Paul II was reported to have worked an exorcism on a man attending one of his masses.)

"What did the priest advise", I asked?

"He looked at me as if I were crazy and actually backed away. He told me I should see a good psychiatrist. These guys can talk a good story, but they don't really believe their own preaching."

"You sound angry," I said, "or bitter. That's understandable but why condemn the priesthood or the church? Maybe your particular priest doesn't believe, or doesn't take it literally, or maybe he does he believe it and it scares him. That would be natural, too."

We pursued the problem no further that day. Chris had a session with me a few days later, and I started to put him into a trance. What happened next was very unsettling. No sooner had he closed his eyes than his voice and demeanor changed markedly. An angry voice issued from him. It was his voice and, yet, it was not. "He's mine!" the voice declared, loud and defiant. As these words came from him, Chris's fists clinched and his arms and legs trembled. His neck stiffened and his lips tightened in an intense snarl, baring his teeth.

Keeping my composure as well as I could, I said in a gentle but firm tone, "Let God's light shine on you and in you. We're all children of God." I had found in the past that when confronted with an entranced patient demonstrating some level of evil, I could dampen the effects by introducing the concept of goodness, specifically alluding to God or to a healing gentle light.

The voice came again, more adamant and foreboding than before. "He's mine. I'm not leaving. I-will-not-leave!"

Valerie Melusky, a psychologist friend of mine had told me of her experiences with such cases. She had written her doctoral thesis on spirit depossession/releasement and had given me some suggestions about handling such situations. Remembering her advice, I told the voice: "Let go of this place where you need no longer be and go into the light. You will be guided there. We all come from God, and no matter how bad we have been, we all get to go back to God, the source of all."

The voice remained defiant and adamant: "I will not leave."

I decided not to press harder, at least for the time being. I told the voice it could rest now, but soon, at the appropriate time, it would be free to go back into the love of God.

I was far from certain what I was dealing with. Perhaps in probing through the surface of a patient who appeared to be simply neurotic I had unleashed a psychotic. Perhaps I was witnessing all the pent-up anger caused by the patient's childhood abuse and pain.

I eased Chris slowly out of trance and spent some time giving him healing affirmations of God's love. When he seemed ready to discuss what had just taken place, I asked him what he thought the voice represented. Whatever it was, he said, he wanted it out and as quickly as possible. So did I, but I wanted to be sure we had any and all appropriate preparations made. A basic rule for good medical care is never to perform an elective procedure without being prepared to deal with its possible complications. If, indeed, spirit releasement therapy was called for, I knew where to find help. With Chris's permission, I phoned Valerie and told her what had transpired. She said it did sound like spirit attachment and offered her assistance.

In preparation, she had two lengthy telephone conversations with the patient and then called me back. We agreed to perform the spirit releasement procedure together and to enlist the help of a nurse who had a deep interest in this field, had had her own psychic experiences, and with whom I had previously worked. There was concern that the patient might experience an intense emotional eruption.

The nurse would monitor the patient's pulse and blood pressure, and if necessary, assist in applying restraints which (again with Chris's permission) I would have on hand. In addition, Chris asked two priests to attend the session, to help or at least be present, but they declined. I must confess that I did not feel confident of success. I had witnessed an alleged spirit releasement only once before, and it had not been especially impressive. I am not sure that much took place except that the patient had received a lot of attention from the five therapists gathered there. Naturally, I was concerned that this might prove to be the case with Chris, and equally concerned that it might not!

The psychologist, the nurse, and I met with Chris in his home. We decided he would be most comfortable in a familiar setting. Afterward, if necessary, he could rest in his own bed. Perhaps he would need a sedative or would at least want to nap.

For two hours, the psychologist merely spoke in a soft voice to him about his problems and about the procedure we were about to undertake. Then she hypnotized him and entreated any attached spirit to identify itself. I am purposely avoiding here any detail of the process. I would not want readers to take this description as a primer for spirit releasement and try to do it themselves.

For some time, she could not elicit a response from the voice I had heard, and about a half an hour passed without obvious progress. Then, at last, Chris spoke in a strange voice. "I am Gregory," the voice announced, "and I am happy here. I will remain."

Quietly but firmly, we debated with "Gregory" about why it was time for him to depart from Chris and go back to the light. The voice argued stubbornly that he had no wish to depart as we continued to firmly urge otherwise.

At one point Chris began to thrash and cough as the nurse continued to monitor his pulse and blood pressure. The voice grew angrier as we persisted.

I readied the restraints and something else that I had brought that might also be effective.

From my bag I took an item which is not regularly issued to medical doctors. It was a small bottle which I had filled with holy water at my church that morning. A lifetime of religious teaching and experience had conditioned Chris to accept the power inherent in rituals such as the sprinkling of holy water, and I felt it might have a favorable effect, a tranquilizing effect if not something more. Of course, I had no way of knowing how "Gregory" would react to it, but with the restraints at hand that was a risk worth taking.

I sprinkled some of the holy water on his forehead and with my finger made the sign of the cross while I talked about peacefulness of spirit and love from God. I wondered to myself what my Jewish grandmother would have thought of my actions. I decided she probably would have said, "Votever voiks."

The thrashing continued briefly and then, quite abruptly, subsided. There was a moment of silence and then, in his normal voice, Chris made a quite unexpected and very welcomed announcement: "It's gone." "Gregory" had left him. A calm seemed to have wafted into the room, perhaps a general feeling of relief. The psychologist asked if there were any other spirits still in habiting Chris. He mumbled that there were six more. We had been at it now for three hours. She had warned me that the procedure could be long, tedious, and messy. All the same, we decided to keep going for a while in the hope of giving Chris total and lasting relief. During the next hour, we addressed the other entities, asking them to identify themselves and urging them to leave as Gregory had departed, into the light. One by one they did so.

I was still unsure of what I had witnessed and participated in. Was it all just a processing of vivid imagination or had seven discarnate spirits of the dead actually freed themselves from Chris's body and gone up into that tunnel of light? Of course, we did not and could not know the answer, nor was one required. This was not a scientific experiment but a therapeutic attempt, and if our patient was better we could be happy with the result.

Chris *was* better. After a year of follow-up therapy he continued to report that the "block" of possession he had felt never returned. After that single session, he had a general peacefulness about him that he never had before.

I encouraged him to find the time each day to "put himself in the light," by way of thanking God and asking for continued peacefulness. After a few weeks he apparently dropped that practice. Three years later I saw him with some new frustrations and anguish with which he is still dealing, but his wife told me that the intense anger had never returned after that releasement session.

Only a few therapists believe that multiple spirit attachment is the explanation for multiple personalities. Others claim it is the other way around, that multiple personality gives an illusion of multiple spirit attachment. Many therapists would argue that neither condition exists.

I would be the first to admit that I do not fully understand all the ramifications of spirit releasement therapy. It would seem to warrant further investigation; however, it needs to be explored carefully. I would not encourage anyone to delve into this process with anything less than the greatest amount of caution. That little angel on my shoulder said, "Let this one go for now, Bob. There are other fish to fry."

Chapter 27

A Father's Pathologic Jealousy

(Some Guys Just Don't Know When to Leave)

Since you've gotten this far without burning or deleting this book, or perhaps sprinkling your e-reader with holy water or garlic juice, you might as well read on. This was a case of spirit attachment and it demonstrated to me in no uncertain terms,

1.) The existence of the spirit

2.) Our ignorance of and inability to know its parameters and machinations, and

3.) The potential dangers in dealing with forces we do not fully understand.

First let me outline some of the working hypotheses about discarnate spirits and spirit attachment. Understand that these explanations are couched and limited to what our minds can conceive and in no way do I presume to explain the mysteries of the universe – but as with all new scientific theories we have to start with some familiar basis. As the name implies a discarnate spirit is a spirit which is not attached to a body (Latin *carnis* - "meat"). When the body dies and its spirit is released, it may go in a number of directions. Many religious and cultural traditions from Judeo-Christian, through Native American, and Tibetan, embrace this basic concept. Hopefully this soul/spirit will be subsumed back into the ubiquitous energy, finding some niche in the balance of the universes' harmony.

At other times the spirit remains earth-bound. It may be because it does not realize its body has died in a sudden and unexpected death. Other cases seem to relate to a persona so strongly committed to a project that it will not leave until that mission is completed. Some spirits stay because they realize what vicious and evil lives they lead and are afraid that if they leave the earthbound realm they will go to a hell. Others crave pleasures they can only experience through a body, and they remain earthbound wanting a functioning body which they can enter and use to again experience their addictions.

Anne was a pleasant, somewhat overweight, single schoolteacher in her late forties. She came into therapy at the urging of two close friends who thought that Anne had anxiety issues about men which always had stood in her way of developing a meaningful heterosexual relationship. She grew up in an impoverished neighborhood in the Southwest, in an extremely dysfunctional family. Childhood memories were rife with brutal episodes of her psychopathic father beating her mother and brother, both of whom committed suicide. As soon as she was able to she ran away from home to the farthest part of the country. Anne denied having any memories of how her father treated her.

I had many patients who had suffered through abusive childhoods and who had blocked out the worst episodes. When something terrible happens to us, we have no trouble consciously remembering it. But when something absolutely HORRENDOUS occurs, our minds protectively push it down below our conscious. The problem is that our emotions still react but without the historical incident on which to hang it. The cure is to go back and remember what happened so as to assign the feeling to its appropriate event, and then relegate it to history and move on. This is where carefully conducted hypnotic regression can be an invaluable therapeutic tool.

We had tried on several occasions to have her recall on a conscious level what had transpired, and to no avail. This was despite that fact that her father had been dead many years. I asked her to relate all the details that she remembered about her father's death, so in that way she would reaffirm that he was dead and no longer able to harm her or anyone else. She said that when he knew he was dying he had pleaded with her to come back and visit him in their old home. She said she hated the thought of doing that but finally relented to his desperation, perhaps hoping this might put an end to her disturbing fears and resentments.

She then described their horrible final meeting. He was wasting away in bed, unkempt, foul smelling, and neglected. He begged her to come closer to him, to sit by his side, and to kiss him goodbye. She felt revolted but pulled up a chair and leaned closer to him. Suddenly he lunged towards her and growled, **"I just want to get into your hair one more time!"** She jumped up and ran out of the room, never to see him again. He died within a few hours.

Anne knew that I practiced hypnotic regression, and without me having to tell her, she knew that was the key to her healing. There was no question that her father had been vicious or that he was dead. The main object now was to have the subconscious accept what the conscious knew. Remembering the historic details and relegating them to history is an integral part of the healing process. The old admonition, "forgive and forget" is erroneous. The way to heal is to "remember and process". Trying to forget is about as effective as trying to not think of elephants – the harder you try, the more it sits in the front of your thoughts.

There is a technique I use to greatly soften the trauma of reliving the repressed experiences, which involves visualizing the incident on a small TV screen which is entirely under the control of the subject to turn on or off. I also give the post-hypnotic suggestion that the subjects upon coming out of trance will not remember any memories they cannot deal with. But that the healing will have begun, and I will know what issues need to be dealt with. Probably the most important concern is to not inadvertently implant false memories. For instance, you would never say, "Go back and see if you were abused". The instructive phrase needs to be as non-directive as possible. For example, I like to say, "Go back to where your REAL problem, REALLY started".

With those parameters, coupled with Anne's resolve to get to the heart of her problem, she said, "Okay, I'm ready. Let's do the hypnosis and get this over with."

We began. I asked her to relax and take some deep breaths in and out. As I continued with the induction she said, "I can't."

"What's the matter", I said?

"He's stopping me."

"Who's stopping you?"

"My father"

"Remember, your father is dead"

"Yes, I'm sorry. You're right"

"Are you ready to start again?"

"Yes"

"Take long slow deep breaths."

"I can't. He won't let me!"

"Who won't let you?"

"My father"

"Okay. Remember your father is dead. You went to the funeral and saw his casket. He can't hurt you anymore. He is dea..."

"GRRRRRR!"

Before I could finish the word "dead" a loud and ominous growl filled the room. We both jumped out of our seats. Anne said, "What was THAT?" Trying to regain my composure I said, "It seems that your father is still around".

I finished the session and we decided that the best recourse to clear up her problem was to do a spirit releasement therapy, for which we scheduled a 2 hour session. The process and goal in this therapy is to have the discarnate spirit realize that if it vacates the host body it will go into the Light, the universal loving, even though it did horrible things when it had its own body. Dr. William Baldwin's book on spirit releasement therapy gives an outline on how to do this. We performed this during the following session.

I do not recommend trying this. I have performed three and would never do them again. Dealing with nasty spirits, and not knowing all the parameters is a scary and dangerous undertaking. It is difficult enough to deal with human physiology and pathology. Wrestling with forces beyond our powers I will leave to whatever clerics or religions that think they can take them on.

More than any other patient encounter, this one unequivocally demonstrated to me that the spirit realm exists. I believe in higher powers, not as a matter of blind faith, but as a matter of cold logic.

Assorted Concepts and Cases

Chapter 28

Mass Hypnotic Regression

Regressions and even past-life regressions and healings can occur in large gatherings as well as in private, one-on-one psychotherapeutic settings. Caution must be taken to not spark the uncovering of emotional problems in a large group of people. However, when I presented a lecture on past-life therapy, I usually include a brief, gently guided reincarnation exercise, and I often concluded with a "healing."

I will share with you a letter I received from a member of the audience at one such lecture. It serves to exemplify the types of experiences a person can have even in a group setting, surrounded by literally hundreds of other people. In fact, many believe that the group atmosphere is an enhancement to healing. This would be comparable to what often transpires in religious ceremonial gatherings, particularly in those at which the acceptance of faith healing is strengthened by the number of people all experiencing and sharing beliefs and reactions.

The woman who wrote to me mentions *Desiderata* in her letter. Her reference is to a short piece of prose written in 1927 by Max Ehrmann, an Indiana poet. I always ended my group meditation with its last paragraph, and I had it printed on the back of my patient appointment cards.

> Dear Dr. Jarmon:
>
> I was one of the more than 450 people in your audience at Virginia Beach last November. Knowing something of the multiple demands ...which impact upon people, I have resisted writing you until this morning. Some spirit suggests that I should go ahead and give you the opportunity of knowing the experiences you enabled this one person to add on her eighty-three-year-old journey.

I have had experiences with guided imagery, meditation, and a range of workshops and therapy. When you started to lead us in the past-life regression imagery using a bridge, my visualization was different from earlier experiences. I was struck by how far away the bridge was, how very long and narrow it was, the sense that I would not have time to reach it and cross it in the time your voice offered. Still, I managed to arrive at the end of it and found I was coming off a crude wooden, makeshift structure. I looked down at my feet and found that I was a very stocky man wearing rough hide, stiff and uncured, cut and folded around my feet and legs, open in the front and tied on my feet and legs ...I was holding a huge club, roaring with anger, facing trees surrounding the area, threatening someone, knowing that I would pound him murderously; at the same time, wary of the danger that lurked immediately behind the trees. Your voice called us back. There is that in me that is very glad to have the sense of primitive rage fully experienced in that body. I have worked through a great deal of anger in different ways in my life, and know myself to be at a very different place today. In some way it was like a gift to be aware of the enormous power existing in that emotional state, and to know that it has been to a considerable extent transmuted in my life experiences. In writing this now, I see that it has helped me voice why I felt the experience as such a gift.

The second event I experienced in some ways of greater importance to me was in your healing meditation bringing us out of the regression. The telling takes longer than the experience.

You had led us in a relaxation and then suggested that we see a beam of white light over our heads. I was experiencing a very strong white light beaming straight down over my head when suddenly a beam of energy/light elbowed its way in at an angle from the side, familiarly like my husband's energy. I was saying in my head, "Oh, Phil, let me have my own image," when your voice began to read and came to, "You are a child of the universe-." Phil died in 1978. One of his favorite sayings was "You are a child of the universe." He cherished the *Desiderata* and had several copies around.

These words on paper cannot begin to communicate the power and synchronicity of the moment, and it was still so funny that I have laughed about it as well. Phil was an extroverted person with an energy field that could make people feel pushed around. I have told a few people who knew him about the experience. We laugh and feel awe at the same time, for it was so characteristic of him. This is to thank you for that gift, too.

Sincerely yours,

Mary Lou Skinner Ross

The following brief passages from *Desiderata,* including its final paragraph, are relevant to the way we perceive ourselves and our experiences, particularly within the context of psychotherapy but also with regard to all of life's experiences:

"Go placidly amid the noise and haste, and remember what peace there may be in silence. As far as possible, without surrender be on good terms with all persons. Speak your truth quietly and clearly; and listen to others, even the dull and ignorant; they too have their story...

Many fears are born of fatigue and loneliness. Beyond a wholesome discipline, be gentle with yourself. You are a child of the universe, no less than the trees and the stars; you have a right to be here. And whether or not it is clear to you, no doubt the universe is unfolding as it should. Therefore be at peace with God, whatever you conceive Him to be, and whatever your labors and aspirations in the noisy confusion of life keep peace with your soul. With all its sham, drudgery and broken dreams, it is still a beautiful world. Be careful. Strive to be happy."

Mary Lou gained a deepened sense of knowing that she did not have before her husband who was so much in love with life, exerts a presence and guidance that has never left her. She need not fear that she will ever be alone.

Chapter 29

S.I.D.S. – Sudden Infant Death Syndrome

In Chapter 14, I related the case of the woman who seemed to have a classic co-dependent relationship with her alcoholic husband, and how she was freed of that by seeing a past-life connection. As she described dying in childbirth, it occurred to me to ask if she had any insight on S.I.D.S. On occasion I have asked questions of patients in deep trance on the chance that while functioning at the super-subconscious level, they might have access to other knowledge.

I said, "Why is it, Cathy, that sometimes an infant will die unexpectedly, for no apparent medical reason? Do you know?"

"Yes, I know," she said. "Sometimes in a rush to return to the earth plane a soul chooses to come into a body and a life that's not the right one to fulfill its karma. After a little while here, the soul realizes its mistake and leaves its new body."

How wonderful, I thought, what a beautiful explanation of S.I.D.S. Surely this understanding could help bereaved parents cope with their grief and begin to accept their loss.

But the world is not that simple and seldom that kind. On the basis of one interview with a hypnotized person, I could not very well imagine some medical journal publishing a paper by Dr. Jarmon announcing to his fellow physicians: "You have all been looking for the wrong causes, allergic reactions or mal-development of the neuronal pathways regulating infant cardiopulmonary response. The truth is so much simpler. The soul finds itself in the wrong body and departs. Stop your research protocols and return your grant money. I have found the mechanism, and it is karma."

No, that is not likely to happen, now or in the future. A truth, an insight, can be a burden as well as a tool of healing. What is to be done with concepts such as this? It is hardly a hypothesis that can be tested by any conventional, widely accepted means. Essentially, it is what is known as a "null" hypothesis: one that can be demonstrated to be true only by eliminating all other possibilities. This would be like having to prove that dragons do not exist by examining every square inch of the universe and not find any. Even that would not prove the nonexistence of invisible dragons, nor is it possible to prove the existence of an invisible concept such as karma and the reality of spirits. Or the reality of the guardian angel, the force, that prodded me to ask about sudden infant death syndrome. Yet, we may be denying ourselves an understanding of our universe by rejecting outright all hypotheses that cannot be tested by orthodox scientific methods.

Most of us retain religious beliefs, in part because we need to believe, to explain to ourselves the inexplicable, and to deal with the prospect of physical mortality; and in part, I think, because we absorb those beliefs in early childhood and they are beliefs shared by our peers. But I am also convinced that all cultures have religious beliefs of one kind or another simply because God does exist and imbues us with belief. Yet, outside of our widely accepted religious concepts, many of us limit our beliefs to those phenomena which can be detected by the five physical senses: sight, hearing, smell, taste, and touch. A blind person has only four senses, a blind and deaf person only three, and a person who has been blind and deaf since birth has to be informed that colors and sounds exist. Being unable to sense them physically does not mean they have no existence. Why should we assume that five is the optimal number of senses? Perhaps we would need ten or more to be fully aware of all that is going on in the cosmos.

For those who profess to heal, it is of enormous benefit to accept and integrate the concept of the soul in treating patients. Good health is not merely the absence of disease but as the more gratifying and fulfilling well-being of body, mind, and spirit. As for life's problems and calamities, they can be viewed as learning opportunities and opportunities for the growth of the soul. That is a much healthier and more productive attitude than cursing the injustice of bad fortune.

The psychotherapist who has some knowledge of the spectrum of psychic experiences and phenomena is in a good position to help a patient separate real from imagined occurrences. I have known patients who suffered needlessly because they were afraid that no one, especially a legitimate therapist, would understand or even believe their out-of-body experiences, near-death experiences, past lives, angelic intervention, or ghostly visitation. Many of these people feared they were losing their sanity. What such people need, I now believe, is a rational approach to the concept of the soul in adjunctive psychotherapy.

This does not mean that we should abandon conventional medicine or psychotherapy. As I said elsewhere, established medical treatment is the basis and starting point. Meditation is no substitute for a needed appendectomy, and an emotional trauma suffered in a patient's present life rather than in a past life is usually the incident that requires the attention.

All the same, the therapist who can work with spiritual concepts while maintaining objectivity and a command of reality can help patients heal in ways that standard psychotherapy does not provide. In this book, I shared some of my experiences in this regard. The most important concept I learned is that our existence is immortal. In medicine, we struggle to keep these temporary vehicles for the soul, our bodies, from breaking down and dying. The truth, of course, is that these vehicles must inevitably fail.

There is enormous benefit to mankind in preventing or curing physical disease, but the *ultimate* focus should be on building a healthy, productive, and learning existence while we are here on this earth plane. Think of it as a school session that is now in progress and will be interrupted, but will also eventually be resumed. Death is only a recess, an indeterminate period of rest and recuperation for the soul. We expend too much anguish over death, and that anguish can be a waste of vital energy. We would do better to focus on life, and accept eventual death as a rest period that will come when it will. Meanwhile, those of us in the healing arts should search for new ways to help our patients when the old modalities have been exhausted and the pathologies persist.

While not risking our patients' well-being, we ought to re-examine our own orthodoxy and our smugly comfortable, conventional attitudes and reverence of mechanistic medicine. Albert Einstein said, "The important thing is not to stop questioning. Curiosity has its own reason for existing. One cannot help but be in awe when he contemplates the mysteries of eternity, of life, of the marvelous structure of reality. It is enough if one tries merely to comprehend a little of this mystery every day. Never lose a holy curiosity."

It is also acceptable to acknowledge that there are many things which we do not know. Thomas Jefferson advised that, "Ignorance is preferable to error; and he is less remote from the truth who believes nothing, than he who believes what is wrong."

My favorite commentary, however, on our arrogant ignorance of the workings of psyches or universes, and the dismissing of others' opinions is found in John Godfrey Saxe's delightful poem based on an old Sufi parable, "The Blind Men and the Elephant."

It was six men of Indostan to learning much inclined,
Who went to see the elephant, (though all of them were blind),
That each by observation might satisfy his mind.

The first approached the elephant, and, happening to fall
Against his broad and sturdy side, at once began to bawl,
"God bless me but this elephant is nothing but a wall!"

The Second, feeling of the tusk, cried: "Ho! What have we here.
So very round and smooth and sharp? To me 'tis mighty clear
This wonder of an elephant is very like a spear!"

The Third approached the animal, and, happening to take
The squirming trunk within his hands, thus boldly up and spake:
"I see," quoth he, "the elephant is very like a snake!"

The Fourth reached out his eager hand, and felt about the knee:
"What most this wondrous beast is like is mighty plain," quoth he.
"'Tis clear enough the elephant is very like a tree."

The Fifth, who chanced to touch the ear, said, "E'en the blindest man
Can tell what this resembles most; deny the fact who can,
This marvel of an elephant is very like a fan!"

The Sixth no sooner had begun about the beast to grope,

Then, seizing on the swinging tail that fell within his scope,
"I see," quoth he, "the elephant is very like a rope!"

And so these men of Indostan disputed loud and long,
Each in his own opinion exceeding stiff and strong,
Though each was partly in the 'right, and all were in the wrong!

So, oft in theologic wars the disputants, I ween,
Rail on in utter ignorance of what each other mean,
And prate about an elephant not one of them has seen!

Chapter 30

The Man Who Would Be Queen

In discussion of reincarnation often the subject comes up of if in a previous life we were of the other sex. According to reincarnation theory, the purpose of living through a sequence of lives is to learn (usually by experience) all there is to know about the human condition. The more we know, the closer we come to omniscience, and the omniscient one, the godhead. So along with many other concepts we need to know and appreciate, we need to know what it is like to give birth as well as to sire an offspring. So, yes, to experience all, we live in different genders.

This answer invites other questions (as most questions do). Are there any gender trait carry-overs from previous incarnations, and would that have anything to do with gender identity disorders? Good question. Let me tell you about Fredrica.

Fredrica was a tall husky 32 year old who came to my office for gender identity confusion. She had been born Fred. Fred grew into a big strong boy but inside always felt that he was a girl. He very well played the role of a big tough guy, but he always knew it was an act. Then came a time in his life when he felt he had to be honest with himself and be what he was always meant to be. He entered a sex change program at a large, prestigious medical center. The center required at least two years of psychoanalysis there before they would enter the sex change operations phase of the process. Fred had completed the entire program, including the surgery, a year before coming to see me. Her problem was that Fredrica still felt that something was very much unfinished.

We talked at length about her life and her feelings, and it seemed that she was a very well integrated and adjusted person except for this one major conundrum. When I was satisfied that for at least the time being there was nothing more to be explored at a conscious level, we began induction for regression therapy. As I almost always did in hypnotic regressions, to be as un-directional as I could I said, "Go back to where the REAL problem, REALLY started". In the first person, she related the following scene, which I will condense.

She was an old woman living in a dirt floor hut, tending the fire and wondering where her son was. She also wondered why he was so brutish and mean to her. Soon the young man came into the hut and yelled at his mother for not having his food ready. She tried to explain and turned back to tend the fire. As she did, in a rage he picked up a fire iron and hit his mother on the right side of her head. She fell to the floor. As the old woman lay there dying she thought, "Why are men so mean? How can they be so cruel? I'll never understand them, NEVER!"

As she saw herself dying there and the life force leaving her body I gave her the healing affirmation that in a future life she would finally learn what it was like to be an angry man and with that her soul's quandary would be put to rest. Additionally any pains that the dying corpse on that dirt floor experienced, would be gone once the life force left it.

When Fredrica came out of trance I asked her how she felt. She said she felt fine, as if a big weight had been lifted, though she remembered hardly anything of what she had said. I asked her if she had ever experienced chronic headaches. She said she had them all her life, very localized on the right side of her head. Numerous doctor visits through the years had failed to find a cause or cure. "But it's not there now! That's great. What happened?" I related what she had said.

It seemed odd that such an intense, lifelong issue could be resolved in a single session. I would have liked to talk with her more at length, but it seemed that there was just nothing more to discuss. I asked her to call me in a week as a follow up and to see how she would fare. She called back as requested and said everything was fine. Her emotional burden had gone as was the head pain. She thanked me very much and I never heard from her again.

That was my one and only case of gender identity treatment. Hardly worthy of an important clinical paper, but one more example of what possibilities exist in a field we really know so little about.

Edgar Casey told of a past life reading he had conducted on a town drunk in Virginia Beach. In the prior incarnation his soul had been in a successful young man whose father was a drunk. The young man died saying, "I just don't understand those damn drunks. My father and all the other bums like him would rather drink themselves to death than be there for their families. I'll just NEVER understand that!"

Karmic philosophy makes a great case for having empathy for the other person and his or her situation. If you fail to appreciate the particular human condition, vicariously, you have to come back and learn it experientially. As the "Duke" said, "We can do this the easy way…or the hard way."

Chapter 31

Shoulder Angel

And some useless tubing

In the early chapters of this book, I described some of my experiences as a medical student and as a young doctor specializing in emergency medicine with experiences that influenced my outlook when I became a psychiatrist. There was another such experience

It began at half past seven on a September morning at Martland Hospital in Newark, New Jersey. I had just begun my third year of medical school and was now in my first week of clinical studies which was in pediatrics. Having transferred to New Jersey Medical College from Guadalajara, Mexico, I was feeling some anxiety about my ability to perform well in this exciting and difficult new environment. The demands of clinical rotations include not only medical knowledge but stamina, vigor, determination, and occasionally a kind of creative initiative.

One of the patients assigned to me was a two-month old African-American baby. She had been severely battered by her mother's boyfriend. Perhaps she had been wet or hungry or suffering from colic when she had begun screaming and could not be quieted, and the man had become furious. He threw her across the room, and her head struck a wall. Jim, the intern in charge of my instruction for this six-week period, had told me to take daily measurements of the circumference of the infant's head. These measurements would provide a rough indication of intracranial swelling from possible bleeding.

On that morning, however, I realized I did not have my measuring tape in my instrument bag. I looked about for something to wrap around the baby's head that later I could measure. I spotted a neonatal (newborn baby) suction catheter, a long, thin piece of clear plastic tubing which when attached to a suction pump, can be used to remove fluid secretions from an infant's nose, mouth, or respiratory tract.

These suction catheters are kept individually wrapped in sterile packets, and they are not inexpensive. At first, I hesitated to waste a catheter to take the measurement, but perhaps because I had much to do and was in a hurry, I decided to go ahead and use it. I removed the tubing from its long, sterile envelope, marked the circumference on it, and then immediately realized that I could have taken the measurement without even opening the sterile bag. I could just as easily have used the long envelope itself, with the tubing still sealed inside it instead of wasting the catheter. I could have taken the measurement and afterwards replaced the bag where I had found it on the nurse's cart. But it was too late, and I had more pressing matters to attend to.

After recording the circumference on the patient's chart, I had no further use for the tubing. I was about to toss it into the trash can when something seemed to tell me to hold onto it. I did not know why, but I felt I had to keep it. I stuffed it into my back pocket and went on about my morning duties.

When I finally was able to sit down for lunch, I felt the now forgotten catheter still in my pocket and thought I had better throw the thing out before my intern saw me walking around with a piece of contaminated equipment sticking out of my back pocket. But as I reached for and grabbed it, once again something told me to keep it. At least six more times during the course of that day, the thought came to me again that for some unknown reason I would need that catheter. It was not until after eleven at night that Jim and I had taken care of all our duties. "Let's go down to the E.R.," he said, "and see if anything's happening."

In the break room next to the emergency cubicle, Jim and I had a cup of coffee and started to chat with the other students, interns, and residents who were on duty. Suddenly we heard a commotion, and a woman rushed past the security guard into our room. She was frantic. In her arms, she clutched a newborn infant who was grunting, struggling to breathe. Jim grabbed the baby and we rushed into the ER cubicle. The child's air passage was obviously obstructed and required immediate intubation, placement of a tube into the trachea which goes from the mouth to the lungs and allows air pass in and out. As quickly as possible, we positioned the tiny infant's head and neck, but when Jim tried to intubate, a delicate and difficult task with a six-pound child, he found the mouth to be full of mucus and vomitus, and he could not see the small vocal cords between which he had to pass the little endotracheal tube. The mouth needed to be suctioned out and very quickly before oxygen deprivation could cause brain damage or asphyxiation.

Jim called for a neonatal suction catheter, but there was none. Someone had mistakenly put only adult catheters on the intubation tray, and the ends were too large to fit the infant-size suction apparatus. By then, the baby had ceased breathing and lay motionless.

As the co-workers around me became frantic, I suddenly realized that I had the life-saving length of tubing in my pocket. As I yanked it out and attached it, it occurred to me that this infant would live because for about 16 hours I had carried this "useless" object that I should have thrown out.

I suctioned the baby's mouth, Jim intubated her, and we admitted her to the hospital. The obstruction had been an infectious swelling. Several days later when the swelling had subsided and been healed by medication, she was discharged in the care of her grateful mother. The other baby, the battered infant whose head I had measured with the catheter, also recovered fully. But it was the baby with the clogged airway who remained most vividly in my mind. She had been saved by a useless catheter.

Either my guardian angel or that baby's, or both were on duty that day.

Many years have passed. The intern who intubated the baby was Dr. James Oleske who went on to gain worldwide recognition as the physician who discovered the link between infants with AIDS and their mothers. Jim and I occasionally worked together as members of the executive board of our alumni association. I think he would agree that some unknown, inexplicable knowing had guided my actions that day when I just could not throw out that catheter.

This concept of divine intervention, or a guardian angel, came up frequently in my counseling work. While some of my patients would laugh at such a notion, many others believed in it or in its possibility. Those patients inclined to believe often found great comfort.

For such patients, the angel (or divine force of intervention, if you prefer) serves as a guardian, spiritual teacher, and confidante. The angel knows more about the patient than does the patient or the therapist and is always present, with the sole mission of helping the patient learn the lessons needed in life. It is a comforting thought, but does it have a basis in reality?

Because so many patients have confided in me about the concept of angels in their lives, I decided to learn more about the subject. I found that many cultures and religions hold to a belief in angels, quite often winged spirits in an otherwise human or partially human form. To the Balinese, they are winged mermaids; to the Vikings, the *Valkyries*; to the Greeks, the *horae*. The Hindus speak of the *Apsaras*; and the Persians of their *Fereshta*. One version or another of this concept is incorporated into such diverse religions as Buddhism, Taoism, Zoroastrianism, Islam, Judaism, and Christianity.

All the same, an average educated person in western society has great and understandable difficulty in visualizing a large, humanoid, winged supernatural creature perhaps evolved from ancient pagan beliefs. To attribute this physical form to the concept is not necessary, however appealing it may be to some individuals and, indeed, to some entire cultures. Consider instead a guiding force.

Perhaps you have had an experience such as driving up to an intersection where the traffic light has just turned green. No other cars are in sight. There is no indication whatever that you need do anything but proceed on your course. Suddenly, for no apparent reason, you slam on your brakes. Perhaps your foot just seemed to move to the brake pedal of its own volition, or you had a sense that you must not drive through that intersection, or you heard or thought you heard a warning voice. A split second later a car, unseen until this instant, darts across the intersection, its driver ignoring the red light. If you had not stopped, you surely would have been hit.

That kind of experience is accepted by many as a case of

angelic or divine intervention. You do not have to see an angel appear in full winged glory to feel its effect.

So if protective angels exist, why is it that accidents still happen? Why don't they always protect us from dangers? The karmic explanation would be that we needed to have that accident as part of our experiences in this life.

You do not have to squelch or hide a belief in this concept for fear of ridicule. George Washington was not embarrassed to speak of an angel at Valley Forge, and others who wrote of angels have included Dante, Milton, Goethe, and the twentieth-century philosopher, Rudolph Steiner. I once gave a talk at a psychoanalytic conference on "working with angels" and my acceptance and use of the concept in my work with those patients who can derive benefit from it. I then polled the audience with regard to any experiences these respected therapists might have had with angelic or divine intervention. Ninety percent responded that they had at least one such experience in their own lives. And, "Thank you", we'll take help from wherever we can get it.

Chapter 32

Healed by an Unknown Entity

This case still puzzles me. I do not know what force or forces were at work. It was one of my first in the realm of spiritual psychotherapy, or as some mockingly call it, "Aquarian therapy".

Martha was a quiet, very pleasant woman in her late fifties. She had grown up in rural Minnesota and remembered many cold, lonely days there during World War II when the men in the area had gone off to war. She had spent some of those years in an orphanage because there was no one at home to take care of her during the day.

Although she had a gently jovial manner, she had sought therapy to relieve what she described as a lifelong sense of "lonesomeness." When I inadvertently referred to her feeling as loneliness, she always corrected me and did so in a mild tone of exasperation that was very rare for her.

"Don't you see the difference?" she said. "Not lonely, lonesome."

I tried without much success to comprehend the subtle difference. A grasp of nuances is, after all, part of the art of psychiatry. I think perhaps her feeling was not quite a sense of isolation but of longing for someone or something unknown. She was married, had a family, and certainly was not alone, isolated, or without the emotional support of loved ones. Still, she felt lonesome and always had. She had been in therapy with another psychiatrist for three years, but he had not been able to relieve her melancholy. He had thought that perhaps another therapist might find a key to her problem, and so she came to be in therapy with me for the summer months.

Most of my patients are in short-term therapy, so Martha's case was unusual for me, unusual and disheartening. I could not say that I had made any more progress than her other therapist with whom I consulted; and I was feeling uncertain how to proceed further. Then one afternoon, in the course of telling me more details concerning her family, she mentioned that her sister had

had a near-death experience. The sister had described it, and Martha believed it fully. I asked her then if she accepted the existence of the soul and the concept that it leaves the body when we die. She said she did.

At the time, I was counseling another patient who was my first to find a resolution of her problems after hypnotic regression and seeing previous lifetimes. Perhaps Martha's problem, too, was rooted in a past life. A further discussion of the soul seemed to be indicated.

I had regressed her under hypnosis many times, and she was an excellent subject to the extent that she always brought a sweater to my office even on hot summer days. She needed to put it on before hypnotic regression because when she went back to her childhood in Minnesota she would shiver with cold.

I now regressed her to childhood, then back into the womb, and then to "Back before that." Her facial expression rapidly changed from peaceful, to puzzled, to astonished. Then she thrust herself forward in her chair, and with her eyes still closed she turned her face toward me and fiercely demanded, "What do you want?"

Her tone and expression were so unexpected and intense that I was taken aback. For a moment I wondered if she might be revealing a multiple personality. But it seemed unlikely that a multiple-personality syndrome could have remained hidden or disguised throughout all of her therapy. All the same, her voice simply did not sound like Martha's as she demanded again, "What do you want?"

I gathered my wits and replied, "I want to help Martha. Will she be all right?"

The persona in my patient's chair moved her head from side to side and then said very firmly, "Martha will be all right." Still uneasy, I asked, "Who are you?"

She said, "I am the angel of peace."

I know I must have hesitated, and I asked the next question falteringly, but I did manage to say, "Are there other angels?"

Again she turned her head from side to side, briskly this time, and then said simply, "Yes."

"Who are they?"

Tersely she said, "It is enough for you to know that Martha will be all right!"

I was perplexed, and hesitated again, but if somehow I was truly communicating with an angelic entity there in my office, I wanted to find out more. Regaining as much composure as I could, I asked, "Where do you come from?"

The question seemed to irritate her. It was as if my questions were somehow improper. Still with her eyes closed, she thrust her face closer as she replied: "I said it is enough for you to know that Martha will be better!"

I decided the time had come to retreat. "Well," I said, "I'm happy that Martha will be well."

I brought the patient back out of trance. Once more I was looking at the woman who had sat down in that chair half an hour earlier, and once more her voice was her own. She did not clearly or fully remember the words of the persona, or mine, but was aware in a general, vague way of the encounter. She was as astonished as I had been and was profusely apologetic.

"What was *that*, Dr. Jarmon?" she said.

I really had no idea. So I said, "Martha, the important thing is how do you feel?"

She thought about it for a brief moment and then replied, "I feel fine, but what *was* that?"

"I have to tell you I'm not sure, but it's not anything to worry about. Let's just see how well you do now."

She made another appointment and, still looking confused, got up to leave.

"What was that?" she said again, shaking her head as she left the office. I phoned her that evening to make sure she was all right. She said she felt strangely different but more importantly the lonesome feeling was gone. It was wonderful she said, to not to feel lonesome any more, as if a great weight had been lifted.

When she arrived for her appointment the following week, she said she had not told anyone what had transpired, not even her husband. She was still feeling great, but also still baffled. "What *was* that?" she repeated. I had no better answer for her than when she had first asked.

We repeated the hypnotic induction and regression, but this time I was better prepared. Aware of her religious beliefs, I held a crucifix in one hand, although I had no idea whether it might help me or be needed in any way in communicating with the patient or with the angelic persona. There was no way to predict even whether the persona would come forward again. I rather expected it to, however, and I was not disappointed. Once more, the transformation took place. Prepared or not, I was still slightly unnerved when the voice demanded, "What do you want *now*?"

"I just want to be sure Martha will continue to be well. She came to me for help, and I need to be sure I've given it and that she'll be well".

I still remember and must confess that as I said those words I felt a little foolish. My concern for the patient was genuine, of course, but even as I was speaking I wondered if my statement sounded as if I were fawning, trying to ingratiate myself with this persona. Perhaps what I had said would further irritate this strange being.

"I told you," she said, "Martha is healed now."

The tone of the voice was firm, but didn't sound irritated. Perhaps I was being defensive and merely imagining the irritation. I decided to venture further, in fact, to ask if my efforts at communication had offended her.

"Are you irritated with me?" I asked. "You seem annoyed."

"You summoned me too quickly."

The voice was intimidating; but it had replied. It had not peremptorily dismissed me, and I began to believe I might be able to initiate a true dialogue.

"May I ask where you come from?"

"Do not ask so many questions. It is enough for you to know that Martha is better."

With that, she leaned forward, closer to me. Martha's eyes were still closed, and yet, I had the feeling this persona was examining the air or perhaps the aura around my face.

"What are you looking for? May I help?" I asked.

"I want to see if you have honesty."

And? What do you find?" I asked with some hesitation.

"There is sufficient."

I realized that further questioning would be futile and might possibly elicit hostility, the last thing I wanted for myself or my patient.

I brought Martha out of trance.

"Dr. Jarmon," she said, "that wasn't me. I don't know who or what that was, and I apologize for whatever came out of my mouth, but believe me, that wasn't me."

I reassured her that I did, and she went on:

"I don't know what happened, but I know I'm different now, and that bad feeling I've had all my life, that miserable lonesomeness, it's gone. I know we're finished now. I want to thank you for what you've done for me. I mean, I know it wasn't you who healed me. It was something else. But you were here like a conduit to let it happen. I feel wonderful now."

A few months later, Martha called just to let me know that everything was fine. She had kept one more appointment with the other psychiatrist because it had been scheduled and he wanted to see how she was getting along. Dr. DiFeo had been very pleasantly surprised at the change in her. I asked her what he thought about her experience in my office with the visitation of the persona, or angel of peace, or whatever it was.

"Oh, I couldn't tell him about that," she said.

"Why not?"

"I wouldn't want my psychiatrist to think I'm crazy!"

Over the next several years Martha would send me a Christmas card each year. She is still well and happy. We still have our little secret, and I still do not know what happened there in my office.

Chapter 33

The Mystified Homicide Detective

One of the reasons that psychic or soul therapy is so slow to be accepted is that it is so difficult to study and document. Modern Psychiatry has a difficult enough time trying to demonstrate that it is on a scientific and vital par with other medical specialties. Consider that the medical postgraduate training for internal medicine, a field with a literally endless amount of information (new findings and studies coming out faster than you can read them all) comprises three years. In contrast, a psychiatry residency requires four years (Everybody duck! Here comes the wrath of the psychiatry establishment).

Psychic experiences are not given to being called up on request, to be studied. Patients have asked for past-life regressions and nothing happens; while others, including hypnotherapists I have known, don't want any part of that, and vivid past-life images break in. Then there are those individuals who experience just one psychic event, but it is profound enough to challenge and change the entire perspective on our mortality.

Several years ago I was giving a talk at a reincarnation conference. Afterwards a gentleman in the back of the room came up to me and asked if we could discuss something in private. He gave me his business card. His name was Robert Snow, and he was a homicide detective in Indianapolis, IN., later to become its chief of detectives. He has since written a book, "Looking for Carroll Beckwith" and was featured on a PBS TV program about the story he wanted to discuss, so I feel free to write about it.

The police department had occasionally used the services of a hypnotist to help find lost clues, and Bob decided he ought to personally vet the woman if they were going to rely on her as much as they did. He called and made an appointment, not giving his real name, and he paid her in cash. As soon as she completed the hypnotic induction, a strange feeling came over him and a strange vision appeared.

He saw himself painting a portrait of an old lady, and simultaneously had feelings of irritation and disgust. He had thoughts something like this, "Why would a woman this ugly want a picture painter of her. I wish I didn't have to do these portraits...but it pays the bills. God how I would love to be in the countryside on a day like this, painting the Seine."

The hypnotist asked him what he was seeing and who he was. Bob replied in the first person that he was Carroll Beckwith, who was a male painter in the 19th century. She then proceeded to ask him details about his life. As "Carroll", Bob proceeded to answer all of her questions. When he came out of trance he felt as if his body had been returned to him and had no idea of what to make of what had just transpired. She told him that spontaneously this sometimes happens with people under hypnosis, and she is not sure what it means either.

For the next two years Bob spent his lunch hours researching Carroll Beckwith and looking in art books for the painting. Some of the painter's personal information was sequestered in a New York City art museum. Of the more than 40 specific pieces of information which Bob had recounted, all but two were found to be true. But in no book or catalogue of paintings could he find a picture of that portrait.

Two years after that one meeting with the hypnotist, Bob and his wife were about to celebrate their 25th wedding anniversary. They decided to spend a few days in New Orleans, a city they had never visited but had wanted to see. After checking into their hotel they decided to explore the neighborhood. With no specific plan in mind, they wandered down one side street and then on to a smaller street. They found themselves outside of an antique store. Bob walked in and there in front of him was the portrait he had been looking for, for two years.

The shop keeper saw the startled expression on Bob's face, approached him, and asked if he found the portrait interesting. The owner then went to his filling cabinet and pulled out the information card on the piece and said that this was painted by a somewhat obscure American artist, Carroll Beckwith. Bob thought the price too high and decided to pass on buying it, later regretting that decision.

Bob was not sure what all this meant, nor what if anything he should do next about the entire affair. He had an important position with the Indianapolis Police Department, which could be jeopardized by his going public with this story which some people might interpret as a sign of instability. In the end he decided that the right and honest course of action would be to share this remarkable experience and let the chips fall where they may.

Sometime later Bob contacted me in New Jersey to say that a small art studio in New York City was going to have a showing of Carroll Beckwith paintings. He and his wife were thinking of coming in to see it and invited me to join them.

He and I went in and found a quiet side room where some of the paintings were displayed. We wanted to see if he could get back into that state of mind or persona of Carroll Beckwith, or any emotional reaction at all. Nothing happened. I then tried to hypnotize him and take him back in time. Again -- nothing.

So what was all that about, and what if anything does it mean. Is Bob Snow the reincarnation of Carroll Beckwith? Was the spirit of Beckwith channeling through or temporarily attaching to Bob? Was it all just an extremely, near mathematically impossible string of coincidences? Or was it all just a made up story and a big run-around created by Bob Snow for whatever reasons? I know Bob, and I know it is not the last possibility. Form your own opinion, and know that you are entitled to it.

Chapter 34

Born to Lose and to Suffer

"Be careful what you wish for."

New discoveries in any field are made along the way, and we continually amend our knowledge base. With something as complex as the human psyche, I cannot imagine ever coming to the point where we can say that now we understand it. Emerson Pugh, PhD, fellow of the American Physical Society and of the A.A.A.S. famously said, "If the human brain were so simple that we could understand it, we would be so simple that we couldn't.

Case in point, there was another patient encounter that reminded me how little we know about what makes us do what we do. A therapist is supposed to help heal a patient's psyche or emotional state. That is certainly a worthy goal and every patient is worth *trying* to help. But maybe we assume we have more power than we do. Perhaps there are patients who are not meant to heal.

I believe Frankie was a patient destined to suffer, tethered to a relentless karma. Sadly he was the kind of person often callously described as a "born loser." Overweight, balding, homely, and bitter, he had grown up in a poor, tough, blue-collar neighborhood in New York. He was extremely passive-aggressive. Once I said to him, "Frankie, you'd spend five hours trying to figure out how to get out of five minutes of work." He perked up and replied, "That's exactly what my last therapist told me"

At the age of thirty-seven, he had achieved nothing worthwhile, and although he had frequent get-rich-quick fantasies, he had no real ambition of any kind. His mother used to tell him that when he was an infant he would habitually lay flat in his crib, doing nothing, hardly moving, and he had not changed much as he grew older. His brother and sister had somehow acquired an attribute which had eluded Frankie, a work ethic.

Some people seem to prosper even without diligence and honesty, but Frankie was not one of them. He was very intelligent and he seemed to possess an evil streak that inspired disreputable schemes, but he was too lazy to attempt to carry out these plots. One day in my office, as he was raging against his lot in life and typically blaming every possible scapegoat from banks to politicians, he exclaimed, "That's it, damn it, I'm going to blow up the f*****g Republican headquarters!"

"How are you going to get there, Frankie?", I asked.

He paused, looked at me with puzzlement and frustration, and shrugged. "Oh, the hell with it," he answered. "The bus probably doesn't go there anyway."

Occasionally, he almost seemed to be mocking himself. One day he burst into my office in an excited state and told me: "Last night I finally figured it out, Doc. I finally realized what's wrong with me. I'm a schizophrenic; I've got two personalities." Then, he suddenly looked crestfallen and almost in the next breath he softly remarked, "No, that's crap, Frankie, we've got it all wrong. That's not it at all." Another time, agitated and frustrated over his inability to accomplish anything, he shouted, "You probably think I'm not doing a f******g thing! I'll have you know I'm burning a hell of a lot of energy just spinning my wheels!"

I believe he enjoyed his sessions with me because they struck him as getting something for nothing. To avoid paying or working for anything had become almost a vocation for Frankie. Seventeen years before I saw him, when he was only twenty, he had been in an accident, hit by a truck. He showed no physical effects, and his injuries probably were minor, but with the help of a clever attorney he had parlayed the accident into financial security, an insurance settlement that would pay for a certain amount of therapy and would support him sufficiently so that he would never have to work again. For whatever reason, he had been deemed emotionally traumatized and unemployable. Of course, the object of his psychotherapy was to get him "back to normal" under the terms of the settlement, a nebulous concept in Frankie's case. If and when the insurer concluded that psychotherapy could not accomplish that, payments for counseling would cease, though other medical expenses would be paid until the day he died.

I tried most every therapeutic modality, and his case became a kind of ultimate challenge to me, but we were making little progress. He seemed to take a perverse pleasure in his own failures. Far from seeking work, he remarked more than once that he actually avoided employment, because if he ever got a job he ran the risk of being fired. He concluded that he was much better off remaining "sick". In fact once he admitted that his worst fear was to be re-evaluated and deemed cured.

Although he held tenaciously to that style of existence, Frankie was one of the unhappiest human beings I have ever met. I saw him as the quintessential example of the adage "Be careful of what you wish for, you might get it!" Frankie had wished to never have to work in life. He had gotten his wish and was miserable. Although he often told me in fits of rage that his hatred and bitterness were bottomless, there was also a tender, compassionate corner of his being. He had wept at the sight of a poor old man, driven to do menial labor for a few dollars a week. Maybe it was his refusal to exert any effort that kept him from being a destructive sociopath, but I think it was his gentle side.

From time to time he remarked, "I must have been some God-awful son-of-a-bitch in my last life to get all this crap dumped on me in this one!" I was not yet experienced in past-life therapy; but nothing else was working for him, and so one day, almost without thinking, I said half-jokingly, "Well, you're a good hypnotic subject. Why don't we go back and see what you did the last time around to deserve such a lot in this life?"

He very quickly went into a deep trance, and I was soon to regret, or at least question, my decision. A horrifying transformation started to take place within the man seated in front of me. A deep hideous laugh roared out of him like human thunder. His face turned red as the blood vessels in his skin dilated and pounded. A snarl came over his face, and saliva dripped from his gaping mouth. Everything seemed to resound with the energy he emitted.

I thought this might be the precipitation or onset of a psychotic breakdown, and I had better return him to his pre-hypnotic state as expeditiously as possible. If Frankie were correct in that he was some reincarnated mega-SOB, some Nazi concentration camp prison guard, I certainly did not want that persona in my office with me!

Heeding Shakespeare's Falstaff's view that discretion is the better part of valor, I brought him out of trance. He looked as if all the energy had been drained out of him in a way that I had never seen before or since. He mumbled, "What was THAT"? I had no answer, but I knew I was not going to take him there ever again. My office was in my home, and later that night my wife nervously asked me what had happened that afternoon that made the entire house shake. That alarming experience was my first real brush with past-life therapy. It is a wonder that I ever attempted it with another patient.

I am confounded by the nature of evil, and some would interpret what happened with Frankie as an example of evil or demonic possession. He was not a candidate for institutionalization where therapy could be conducted in a more controlled environment. He would not have gone voluntarily, and other than provoking him, he would not have been seen as a danger to himself or to others.

In conducting past-life therapy and observing some of the astonishing cures that often result, I still often wonder about my role in the therapeutic process. If at least some current-life problems really are a penance for previous-life transgressions, who are we to defy or attempt to bypass that destiny? Not an excuse or rationalization for failing to help a patient heal, but maybe therapists only serve as keepers of the keys at the patient's prison gate. We are there to open the gate when the transgressor has paid his or her debt. We would like to let everyone out when they wanted, but that decision is not really up to us.

Frankie eventually dropped out of therapy when the terms of his insurance settlement dictated that he would have to pay for sessions himself. By then, his rages were less frequent, although he was certainly not cured. He had always wanted to not have to work or to have to deal with people. He wanted no responsibilities whatsoever. In the end all of those wishes were fulfilled. His landlady found him dead alone in his one room garage apartment. He was 42 years old.

I later explored past-life therapy in much more benign settings and utilized it with some remarkable results. I learned from painful experience to heed that inner voice that tells me when to step back. I was a therapist, not a magician, and Frankie had to ride out his destiny without me.

Chapter 35

Cost Effective, Under Utilized, Adjunctive Therapy

In 1988, in the coronary care unit of San Francisco General Hospital, a study was undertaken on nearly 400 post-heart attack patients over a ten-month period. An old and long abandoned adjunct to medical therapy was re-instituted to see if it could improve patient outcome. The patients were divided into two groups such as to give both an equal balance as per the severities of their conditions.

The results were astounding. The group that received the adjunctive therapy as opposed to the control group had significantly improved outcomes as measured by incidences of complications such as congestive heart failure, cardiopulmonary arrest, pneumonia, need for diuretics, antibiotics, and intubation/ventilation. Whereas 7% of the patients in the control group went into cardiopulmonary arrest, only 2% in the *extra* therapy group did so.

The study was conducted under strictly controlled "double blind" guidelines, meaning that neither the patients nor their doctors and nurses knew who was getting the added therapy and who was not.

However, this apparently remarkable aid to patient recovery has several aspects which currently hinder its widespread use. Those are that it is not subject to FDA approval, not expensive, not painful, and not new. Neither does one need a license to administer it nor for that matter to be in the patient's presence during administration!

If this *were* an FDA-approved, eighty-dollar-per-dose, painful, newly developed injection showing these incredible results, physicians would be sued for malpractice for not prescribing it.

Just what was this incredible something? It was prayer.[9]

What was the nature of the therapeutic process at work? Did the minds of those doing the praying connect with their own souls, which in turn connected with the souls of the cardiac patients, which in turn affected physical changes in those patients' bodies? Who can say? But if it worked so well and is so safe and cost effective, why are we not using this more?

There exists a great reluctance in modern medical science to deal with factors affecting patients' well-being which may elude quantification, predictable access, or simply understanding. We see ourselves as keepers of the gate of modern science, believing that whatever is contained within is almost all that should be allowed in. We scrutinize closely (as we should) any pretenders to that body of knowledge. (I would hate to think that our reluctance might stem from our delicate egos. Could we be so threatened at some deep level over the fact that our patient's $4000-a-day services in a modern coronary care unit mean nothing if that patient's little boy is not praying for him at home?)

Fortunately we do not have to make an "either/or" decision here. We can have the best of both worlds. We can and should keep modern medical modalities in diagnosing and treating diseases of the mind, the body, and the mind/body. But we can and should still concomitantly incorporate that elusive intangible that is very much a part of our universe. It stands to reason that if a person's illness is a compilation and amalgam of mind, body, and spirit, that to not address one or two of those factors is to fall short of giving our patients the best possible care.

---

[9] Randolph Byrd, "Positive Therapeutic Effects of Intercessory Prayer in a Coronary Care Unit Population," *Southern Medical Journal*, July 1988, Vol. 81, pp. 826-829.

Chapter 36

When Religion, Hypnosis, and Counseling Met

"These days, if you don't believe in miracles,
you're not a realist."
(Anwar Sadat, on the occasion of Israeli Egyptian peace accords)

All of the encounters and accounts in this book really happened, including the darker ones. I'd like to finish with one of the more positive stories. Perhaps there is something to angels, saints, and miracles.

Angela was a patient I had been seeing intermittently for about three years. Initially, she had come to me for help in breaking her nicotine addiction. She was a middle-aged woman, quiet, trusting, and pleasant, and after a single session she had no difficulty in quitting smoking.

For several months afterward, she made appointments every two weeks or so, to get help in losing weight and to talk about a more distressing worry. Her family life had never been entirely happy. Her husband was a good enough sort, but not very considerate or attentive. Three of her children had somehow failed to acquire a healthy appreciation of the work ethic. But her deepest concern was about her first, the eldest, Maria, a wonderful person who had always been a source of pride and happiness but whose health had been a torment.

Maria had been born with a congenital defect in her renal system and now, at the age of thirty-five, was beginning what would probably be the last year of her life unless she could obtain a kidney transplant. With the deterioration that had already occurred, she was no longer considered a prime candidate for a donor kidney. Angela was visibly distressed, but seemed to accept her lot in life as God's will and was timid about any kind of introspection that might question her belief system. When I attempted to probe deeper into her psyche, she stopped coming to me for counseling.

Then one day she phoned again and asked if she could see me that same day. She sounded almost frantic. Her daughter, Maria, who was living alone in California, had taken a turn for the worse. Angela was going to fly out early the next morning to see her. It was after two o'clock when I received her call, and my day was booked solid with patients for the rest of the afternoon and most of the evening. Several of those patients needed counseling almost as urgently as Maria did. I told her I was very sorry that I had no more openings that day, but would try to work something out and call her as soon as possible. Then I looked again at my appointment ledger and case notes to see if there was anyone I could change.

I had not yet made up my mind when, a few minutes later, my 4:00 PM patient called to say that because a heavy rainstorm had begun, she was afraid to drive to my office and would like to postpone her appointment. I called Angela. She must have been sitting by the phone waiting, because she answered at the first ring. She would be at my office at four.

Shortly before she was due to arrive, my telephone rang again. It was a friend of mine, Jim, a Roman Catholic priest from Pennsylvania. He had driven in for the day to visit a colleague at the local rectory. Jim had lately been struggling with feelings of isolation and frustration, a not uncommon occupational hazard. Today he was feeling especially depressed. He was at an age when many priests have their own parishes. Although he was a kind, gentle, hard-working man, he was becoming resentful, even bitter, over what he regarded as the casual and callous treatment by the diocese that had passed over his requests to become a pastor.

Two months earlier, instead of giving him the parish that the grapevine had told him he would finally get, they had reassigned him from the church where he was assisting to a pastoral-care ministry. Now, over the phone, he was venting some of his anger.

"You know, Bob," he said, "it really rubs salt into the wound, giving me this station. It isn't that I don't want to help these people. I know they need help, but that's not what I feel my calling is. The personnel office never considers the needs of the priest. We're people, too. They don't even seem to care about my health. They know I've got some physical ailments and now they're giving me a job with no support or backup. I'm on call twenty-four hours a day, working maybe sixteen hours at a clip and getting complaints that I'm not seeing everybody who asks for the priest. It's easy enough for any priest to remind himself about praying for guidance and strength, but I tell you this time I feel like I just can't handle the job."

I tried to think of something comforting to say. All I could muster was, "I certainly understand how you feel, but isn't it gratifying to work with people who are looking to the Church for comfort, perhaps for the first time in their lives? Doesn't that feeling of accomplishment help some?"

"Not right now." he said, "Sure these people need someone, but why me? I'm getting to understand better and better how Job felt. These people just want me to give to them, and give, and give. This is a terrible thing for a priest to say, but I'm *tired* of giving. I need to get as well as give. I need it just as much as they do. What I want to know is, when do *I* get?"

A question like that almost defies an answer. How does one respond to a rhetorical question that amounts to a cry for help? A glib reply is no help at all. I hesitated and Jim uncharacteristically said angrily, "Well, thanks for listening," and hung up.

At least for the present, there was nothing I could do, and when Angela arrived I made a conscious effort to put Jim out of my mind and focus on my attention on her problems alone. She began by telling me that her daughter's condition was rapidly deteriorating, and she might not live until Christmas.

"Why is this happening to us?" she said. I've tried to be a good person, a good wife, and mother. I pray to Saint Anthony, but I never get any answers. If my patron saint can't help me and God won't, who's left? I pray, and Maria just gets sicker."

This was another rhetorical question amounting to an anguished cry for help, and again I had no answers. I had nothing to offer except a sympathetic ear. My batting average was not having a great day.

"Angela," I said, "I don't have any more answers than you do.

These things are beyond our comprehension, but I wouldn't stop praying. If we don't seem to be getting any answers, maybe we need to try asking in a different way. While you're here, why don't we try some hypnotic relaxation and meditation and turn all of these questions over to your guardian angel?"

That might sound like strange guidance from someone trained in medical science, but given Angela's strong religious background I hoped that an act of faith might give her some enlightenment or support. It was worth a try.

She quickly slipped into the trance state. Before I could offer further suggestions or ask any questions, she grimaced, then looked puzzled, then pained, then relaxed again deeply. After a moment she smiled fleetingly and began to sob, "My God," she cried, "That's why. Dear God, I'm sorry, I'm so sorry!"

My curiosity rivaled my surprise and relief. "Angela," I said, "tell me. What is it? What is it you see?"

Still in trance and sobbing, she continued, "The abortion, the abortion! Of course, it was the abortion. How could I be so stupid? Why didn't I understand? It was the abortion. Oh, dear God, forgive me."

"The abortion? Tell me about it, Angela. Tell me about the abortion."

"It was forty years ago. Three months before our wedding. Our families were Catholic and I was eighteen and pregnant. We just couldn't tell them. We were so scared. We just didn't know what else to do. What a terrible decision. It was just as bad for him. My God, how we've regretted it. Forty years and we've never even talked about it, not once. My God, forgive me. I've never told another living soul."

Realizing what her belief system was telling her, I replied, "Yes, Angela, but now you've paid that debt, paid it over and over all these years. You've paid a debt of suffering for the sin, but you've suffered enough, and now that you understand it, you can be at peace with yourself."

After I took her out of trance, she had no difficulty talking about it to me, the first person she had ever told. It was as if her shame had at last been lifted, as if she had been chained by secrecy and was now released.

"You know, Doctor," she said, "I've done my best to be a good Catholic ever since then, and I've raised my children that way. I've made every sacrifice to God and Saint Anthony that I could think of, but there's one thing I haven't done, the most important thing, a part of the debt I *haven't* paid. I never confessed that abortion to a priest. My greatest sin and I never confessed it. Every time I went to communion, I went with sin in my soul." Answers were beginning to come to me as well as to Angela.

"Would you like to receive the sacrament of confession before you see your daughter tomorrow?", I asked.

"Yes. Yes, but the plane, there's no time."

I picked up the phone and dialed the rectory where Jim was visiting. "Father Jim," I said, "I know how much you've been giving, but I need a favor and I'm going to ask you to give again. I need you for an ecclesiastical consultation with a patient of mine who needs confession. And she needs it right now."

"Sure," he said, "Why not? Send her over."

When Angela returned from California, she called me. "That Father Jim is wonderful. We talked for almost an hour. I don't know how to thank you for sending me to him. At the end he said he had no penance to give me, that I'd been doing my penance for the last forty years. I feel so relieved now, I can't explain it. It's, well, a peaceful feeling where a burden was. Whatever happens to Maria, I know it's *God's* will, but you know, I have a good feeling about the future. You can call it faith or whatever, but it's just a good feeling."

Several months later I received another call from Jim.

"Bob, I wanted you to be one of the first to hear the news. I'm getting a parish. It's not very big and it's poor, perfect for me. There's lots of potential for some good solid work. It's just what I was hoping for. And I got a beautiful note from the bishop, would you believe that? He said he knows how hard I worked at my last assignment; he said I left a wonderful legacy of good feelings about what the Church can do for the people." Jim went on to say that his perspective on his counseling ministry assignment had changed after his talk with the woman I had sent to him. "I think you sent her over as much to heal me as to heal her".

I had.

A few days later it was almost Christmas, and I was counseling a patient who was struggling through holiday depression. There was no way for him to know it, but I too was feeling despondent. That Christmas season was a very sad one for me. During the same week when Angela and Jim had sought my help, my mother had died, and this would be my first Christmas without a parent.

Just as the patient was leaving, the telephone rang. It was Angela.

"Dr. Jarmon," she said, "a miracle has happened. Maria got her kidney transplant! This is going to be the best Christmas of our lives. Do you believe in miracles? I hope so. Somehow, I think you had more to do with this than you realize, and I want to thank you. I can't thank you enough. God bless you, doctor, and have a very Merry Christmas."

Epilogue

I hope the day soon comes when psychiatry expands beyond its current limited borders to embrace and provide some of the healings described in this book. It would help if clinical hypnosis were more widely used. Regression hypnoanalysis can help recover deeply imbedded subconscious material while greatly reducing the paralyzing fear of doing so. The anxieties for which many need treatment, are the very conditions which prevent them from talking to a therapist. Psychotherapy can be extremely threatening. I think of the movie, "The King's Speech" in which King George VI's fear of psychotherapy stops him from getting to the root of his stuttering, hindering his ability to speak to his subjects with confidence. While young British R.A.F. pilots were dying overhead fighting the German Luftwaffe, their king was too afraid to examine his childhood.

There were pros and cons to my tangential entrance into the practice of psychiatry. But not having to unlearn some constricting concepts was often a plus. I again think of Jefferson's quote, "He is less remote from the truth who believes nothing than he who believes what is wrong."

I offer two suggestions for psychotherapists after reading this book. If you don't use the concept of the soul in your therapy, at least give space and respect to those colleagues and patients who do. And if you do use it, do not be too cavalier. We do not know the extent of the depth and power. Remember the fate of *Icarus,* the character in Greek mythology whose father made him a set of wings so that he could soar. He ignored his father's warnings about having hubris. When Icarus tried to fly up to the sun (the *Power*), his wax wings melted and he fell back down to earth.

On a personal level, clinical experiences have shaped my perspective on life. I see this lifetime as one very interesting semester in this university of the universe. Some people try to understand why an all-loving, all-forgiving God would condemn them to burn in hell eternally for committing some religious "foot-fault" before they die. We are just here learning. Every problem or new situation is simply another homework assignment, not meant to punish, but to provide a learning exercise.

One day the Headmaster will come and release us from school with a message akin to, "You have done enough for now. Go take a well-deserved vacation. Rest, heal, and before you come back, do some reflecting on what it is that you need to work on next time." Of course, if we learn enough this time around, we may not have to come back at all.

About the Author

Robert Jarmon, M.D. retired from thirty years in clinical practice to devote his efforts towards developing medical devices for the physically disabled.

Made in the USA
Middletown, DE
30 October 2017